Gene Shelburne

# HOMES THAT LAST

## CHRIST'S MESSAGE FOR FAMILIES TODAY

GENE SHELBURNE

Printed and Bound in the
United States of America


***www.covenantpublishing.com***

P.O. Box 390 Webb City, Missouri 64870
Call toll free at 877.673.1015

Library of Congress Cataloging-in-Publication Data

Shelburne, Gene, 1939-
Homes that last : Christ's message for families today / Gene Shelburne.
p. cm.
ISBN 1-892435-52-7 (hardcover)
1. Family--Religious life. I. Title.
BV4526.3.S54 2004
248.4--dc22

2003026758

*To my dear wife Nita,*
*whose sense of humor and godly good sense*
*have made our own family*
*my greatest blessing*

# TABLE OF CONTENTS

DO YOU WANT A SOLID,
HAPPY, ENDURING HOME?

BUILD THE RELATIONSHIPS
IN YOUR FAMILY ON THE
INSTRUCTIONS OF JESUS
IN MATTHEW 5–7.

# PREFACE

"Pastor, please don't lead the Lord's Prayer," the warden for the juvenile center requested. Then he explained to the visiting minister, "Over 80 percent of the kids in this facility were badly abused by their fathers. They don't think what you and I think when we pray, 'Our Father.'"

This surely must seem unthinkable to those of us who have been blessed with godly parents. But during my years of ministry I have learned that even in the best of homes, our deepest wounds tend to be those inflicted on us by family members. And our deepest regrets almost always focus on mistakes we feel we have made in relating to our parents or in raising our own kids.

What does Jesus have to say to us about hurts like these?

All of us get hurt at home, but many of us still would say that we have no greater source of happiness than our families. We're like the athlete who beams into the TV camera and says, "Hi, Mom!" Half the joy of any accomplishment in our lives comes from sharing that victory with those who love us most. At this stage in my own life, any honor I receive evokes deep inside me a silent wish that my mom and dad were still alive to know I got it. Part of the potential joy is missing because they are not here to rejoice with me.

President George W. Bush's top adviser Karen Hughes rocked the White House when she told her boss she was quitting the most influential job in Washington, D.C., to be with her family in Texas. Her critics were dumbfounded. They imagined all sorts of off-the-record explanations for her departure. Karen Hughes told them simply, "I made a decision to do what is best for me and my family." What a wise lady! What a courageous choice!

All of us value our families. Even when those families are far from ideal. Adopted kids often seem to be obsessed with the need to meet their real parents and to know if they have actual siblings. Stories abound of parents who were separated from their offspring by poverty, war, or tragedies of other sorts. These parents spend so much of their time and energy searching for their sons and daughters and wondering what might be happening to them.

What does Jesus have to say to those of us who delight so totally in our families?

## A GREAT GULF

Unfortunately, not all of us share that delight.

Karl Marx based his world-changing political theories on the assumption that the most basic difference between people is poverty and wealth. He discerned that the haves and the have-nots will be forever locked in an eternal struggle.

Horace Mann was convinced that the great dividing line in every culture is the line between ignorance and education, so he poured all his energies into creating a free education system for America's children.

The opinion of another fellow convinces me that he was not a young man. The greatest dividing line in humanity, he said, is not racial color, or political views, or economic status. The biggest difference of all, he insisted, is between those who are forever sick and those who are in good health.

That last observer of life is not far from the Kingdom. But in my own forty-plus years of ministry I have noticed another profound difference in the people I have known and served—a difference that defines who we are and shapes what we can become. Often I have been at a loss to explain why this disparity exists, but the fact that it does exist and that it impacts peoples' lives as profoundly as any other factor is beyond dispute. I am talking about the massive difference in the way we perceive our families.

Why is it that one large group of men and women will tell you in an instant that their families are the source of their greatest grief and woe, while their neighbors are just as quick to point to their families as their single greatest source of happiness and blessing?

How do we explain the great gulf between people with positive-family and negative-family views? We find these folks—so different from one another—living neighbor by neighbor on the same block, sitting side by side on the same church pew, working desk by desk in the same office. On the surface you would think that people growing up in the same social setting would turn out about the same, wouldn't you? But it doesn't work out that way. Some of my friends shudder as they describe nightmarish experiences in their early family life. I have other friends who beam as they give God thanks for halcyon years in homes that were healthy and wholesome and fun. One group has almost totally negative memories of home. The other group's recall of home is predominately positive. What causes this drastic difference?

Is there a greater social division than the line between those of us whose families are a blessing and those whose homes are a curse?

Which one is yours?

No human being should have to grow up in some of the homes I know about. Headlines tell us of mothers drowning their tots or selling them for drug money. But down the scale from this level of egregious criminality and therefore more likely to escape public notice are the thousands of homes

polluted with hate,

terrified by rage,

poisoned by vicious language,

degraded by indecencies,

hamstrung by addictions, and

forever kept off balance by wrong decisions made by parents and children alike. Homes like this are made in hell. Far too many people are stuck in them.

Those of us who grew up in safe, good homes are often aghast to learn that some of our friends grew up in the other kind. I suspect that those who are presently struggling to survive in devilishly destructive homes find it just as hard to believe that other people just like them actually go home to solid, happy homes that provide contentment and stability and fun.

All of us can see that the difference between people with happy homes and hellish homes is huge. What would you say if I told you that most of what we need to know to turn bad homes into good ones can be found in Jesus' famous teachings in the Sermon on the Mount? I know I risk the rebuttal that such a suggestion sounds simplistic, but I hope you'll bear with me at least a few chapters while we explore this premise.

## HOMES THAT LAST

You may discover that the truths Jesus offers us in this great sermon are anything but simple. They probe the depths of humanity's more urgent hurts and needs and can help us avoid many of life's biggest mistakes.

Do you want a solid, happy, enduring home? Build the relationships in your family on the instructions of Jesus in Matthew 5-7. Was the home you grew up in atrocious, or is your present family mired in misery and torn by tensions? Trace most of your troubles to a failure to do what Jesus tells us to do in this single sermon. I know this sounds too simple, but it works out with an uncanny accuracy.

## THE RIGHT PLACE TO DIG

Back in my adolescent days when I practiced my juvenile sermons on anybody who would allow me to afflict them, my rudimentary method of putting together a sermon was what we call prooftexting. State an idea. Quote a verse or two of Scripture that seem to support it. State another idea. Recite another passage. On and on, ad nauseam.

During that immature stage of my ministry, I was invited on several occasions to speak at special gatherings for Christian families. Any message I gave was expected to deal with some aspect of home life and family relationships. Those invitations always put me into a bind because the New Testament does not contain that many overt exhortations to families. After Ephesians 5-6, Colossians 3, and Titus 2, a novice Bible student like me had just about exhausted the obvious texts on the subject.

Today I know better, of course. Having grown up in a great home, married a top-notch wife, raised with her an enjoyable family, and learned the hands-on delight of grandparenting, I now realize that virtually every verse in the Bible shines some rays of light on the fine art of living in our homes. Now I know that although Jesus may not address us by name or title, his teaching is loaded with admonitions to us as husbands, fathers, wives, mothers, if we just listen to him from that perspective.

Most of us, for example, have read or heard the Sermon on the Mount more times than we can count. But how many of us have come to our Lord's best-known teachings for no other purpose than to quarry stones on which to build a healthy, happy home?

Some time ago I set out to read our Lord's famous Sermon on the Mount, asking myself, "What does Jesus have to say in this sermon that would apply to me as a father, as a husband, or as a son? What is Christ's message here for my family?"

The result is the book you now hold in your hands.

GENE SHELBURNE
March 2004

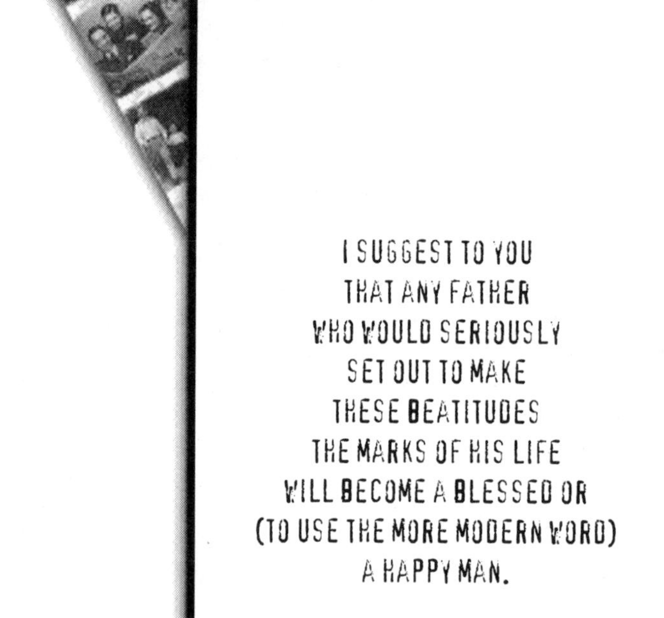

I SUGGEST TO YOU
THAT ANY FATHER
WHO WOULD SERIOUSLY
SET OUT TO MAKE
THESE BEATITUDES
THE MARKS OF HIS LIFE
WILL BECOME A BLESSED OR
(TO USE THE MORE MODERN WORD)
A HAPPY MAN.

**CHAPTER ONE**

# THE HAPPY FATHER

*Seeing the crowds, he went up on the mountain, and when he sat down his disciples came to him. And he opened his mouth and taught them, saying:*

*"Blessed are the poor in spirit, for theirs is the kingdom of heaven.*

*"Blessed are those who mourn, for they shall be comforted.*

*"Blessed are the meek, for they shall inherit the earth.*

*"Blessed are those who hunger and thirst for righteousness, for they shall be satisfied.*

*"Blessed are the merciful, for they shall obtain mercy.*

*"Blessed are the pure in heart, for they shall see God.*

*"Blessed are the peacemakers, for they shall be called sons of God.*

*"Blessed are those who are persecuted for righteousness' sake, for theirs is the kingdom of heaven.*

*"Blessed are you when men revile you and persecute you and utter all kinds of evil against you falsely on my account. Rejoice and be glad, for your reward is great in heaven, for so men persecuted the prophets who were before you"* (Matthew 5:1-12).

How many times have I read these verses we call "The Beatitudes"? Hundreds of times, surely. Only God knows. I know these famous lines are our Lord's divine definition of genuine happiness. But I purposely looked at them this time from a new angle, and a fresh idea struck me.

Surely, I thought, the Beatitudes must supply us the finest description I could find in all the word of God of a really happy father.

After many years in ministry I am acutely aware that many fathers are not happy. For them home is a burden, marriage is a bad trip; children are a liability from the day they are conceived.

If such men perform as fathers at all, they perform grudgingly.

They are not fun to be around. No child could enjoy having them as a father.

If they go through the motions of fatherhood at all, their performance is ninety-nine percent negative.

One day a 50-year-old banker called and asked me to visit with him. As we talked in his office that afternoon, he told me, "The four years just past are the first years of my adult life when I have been happy."

As I left his office, I hurt inside. "That's tragic," I thought. "This person has just told me that for almost half a century he has not been happy."

Maybe this is why so many marriages seem to dissolve almost unexplainably—a pervasive unhappiness shrouds the lives of so many people. As they find themselves locked into a web of relationships they resent—relationships to mates and children who make demands upon them—many fathers today just split. They have enough money to do it. And society no longer frowns upon them for bailing out. Not like it once did. So these unhappy fathers leave, pursuing a happiness which usually eludes them, because they take their unhappiness with them wherever they go.

## REAL HAPPINESS

Jesus begins the Sermon on the Mount by describing a person who is truly happy. Instead of saying, "Blessed are the poor in spirit," and, "Blessed are those who mourn," Today's English Version translates, "*Happy* are those who know they are spiritually poor," and "*Happy* are those who mourn."

Jesus is setting forth here the kind of attitudes and values that will give a person the deep-down contentment and satisfaction with life that all of us long to possess but some of us never find.

I suggest to you that any father who would seriously set out to make these Beatitudes the marks of his life will become a blessed or (to use the more modern word) a happy man.

D. Martyn Lloyd-Jones wrote a two-volume classic on the Sermon on the Mount. It took him one whole volume just to get through the Beatitudes, since he used a full chapter for each of the "blessed" statements of Jesus. Had he kept going at that pace he might have needed twenty-six volumes to discuss the entire sermon.

Dr. Lloyd-Jones has gone now to be with the Lord. The two books he did write on Jesus' great sermon contain the richest material I have found on the subject. He was a capable expositor of the Scriptures, and he saw the Beatitudes of Jesus as *the* description of Christian spirit and Christian life. He felt that any person who could understand and live up to them would have become what Jesus aspires for us to be.

But that grand old English preacher hastened to say that in his opinion no part of Jesus' teaching is more misunderstood than these early verses in Matthew 5. In fact, he said, no part of the teaching of our Lord is probably more difficult to understand than the Beatitudes.

If he's right, in this brief chapter we are not likely to exhaust the meaning of our Lord's Beatitudes, but let's look at them to see how they apply to those of us who are fathers.

## THE POOR IN SPIRIT

What is Jesus talking about when he says, *"Blessed (or happy) are the poor in spirit,"* if he is talking about the role of a father?

Certainly poverty of spirit does not imply weakness of personality, does it? Yet I fear that many who read this first Beatitude conclude that if a man is "poor in spirit," he lacks confidence and boldness. He is not courageous or outgoing.

This is *not* what Jesus means. He is describing strength of personality, not weakness.

What word would you use to define "poor in spirit"? Humility? Yet, in our world *humility* is not a term of honor. When we say, "This man came from humble beginnings," we are not praising him. We mean that he was raised by poor folks, don't we? By the world's standards, this is negative.

When I think of humility, I think of the strength of character that makes a man so confident in his relationships that he does not have to prove anything. So many of the hurts I see in families I counsel are hurts inflicted by a daddy who thinks he has to talk a little louder, stand a little taller, stomp a little heavier to prove to his kids that he is the boss of the family. Sometimes he abuses his wife—verbally if not physically—because he is obsessed with proving to her that he is the "head of the house." Thus in his own inner insecurity, the man fails to possess the poorness of spirit Jesus recommends here.

How can such a man be comfortable with himself when he knows his wife is smarter than he is (which is the case for most of us guys)? What if he raises children who grow up to be clearly more knowledgeable than he is about certain things? If he is driven to prove to them that "father knows best," he is likely to make a mess. Men who are "poor in spirit" don't have to bear that burden.

A man who is poor in spirit has "the kingdom of heaven," Jesus assures us. A father is coming near to what Jesus stands for—he is taking a proper place in the world Jesus runs—when he possesses this special gift of being poor in spirit.

## THOSE WHO MOURN

Then Jesus says, *"Blessed are those who mourn, for they shall be comforted."*

In what sense can we describe a mourning or grieving person as a "happy" person? Rationally this doesn't make sense, does it? Yet Jesus tells us, "Happy is the person who has grief." Our Lord's words here require some scrutiny.

I remember a family who sat in my study one day. They had come to see me several times before. We had been talking about how to help them curtail the illegal drug habits of their beautiful, brilliant 18-year-old daughter. At one point in a hot exchange I remember looking over at this girl's affluent, successful, highly respected father. Tears were streaming down his face.

His high-octane daughter was soon to be a freshman on a university campus known for its high level of drug use. Adamantly this girl refused every request made by her parents. As this man saw his daughter's life about to go down the tubes because of her disobedience to him, he sat there and wept.

I wondered at the time how that girl could see her father's tears without being melted by the realization, "He loves me enough to cry!"

Today she is straight, I think. I hope so. If she is, it is not because of any wise thing I said to her. It is because of the tears of her daddy.

The Bible says that if a person is able to mourn—if they can have genuine, sensible grief over the heartaches of life—they will be comforted. If this girl is drug-free today, her parents have realized this promise.

Show me a man who does not care enough about his own kids to be cut in the heart when they are not good and I will show you a man on the way to misery. Show me a father who does not have enough tenderness of heart to weep before his children—who is too macho ever to let his kids see a tear in his eye—and I will show you a father who is not much father. He is not a happy man.

## THE MEEK

*"Blessed are the meek,"* Jesus said, *"for they shall inherit the earth."*

I suppose more cartoons have been done about this one statement than about anything else Jesus ever said. "Who wants to inherit the mess the earth is in, anyway?" the cartoonists sometimes imply. Others question the basic idea that anybody would want to be meek in the first place.

This business of meekness is deep water. Are you a meek person? Do you have a clear enough idea about what it means to be meek that you can apply this Beatitude to yourself? Is Jesus talking about you when he says, "Blessed are the meek?"

Meekness is the opposite of what we're hearing about in assertiveness training. Some corporate execs are immersed in seminars teaching them to be assertive—in other words, to be pushy. To be aggressive. You need to know how to shove in life and how not to be shoved, they are taught.

A meek person is not a shover. When you are around a meek person, you don't have to wonder if he's going to bulldoze you or berate you or high-pressure you into a position you don't want to occupy. Meek people are not pushy.

Rather than trying to define meekness, let me explain the word by pointing to certain people I know who are meek. They are the best definition I know.

On one occasion I sat late into the night in the home of a Christian man who is meek. Although I had heard him praised as a man of high integrity and deep faith, I had not met him before that day. Now I know why he is so highly esteemed.

He is the sort of man who allows the other person to have his space, but in doing so he doesn't give up his own. He is not a weak person at all. Far from it. But he lets you be you. He doesn't pass judgment on you. You never feel that he is critical of you, but at the same time you have the sure feeling that he knows exactly what he thinks and where he stands. He is not namby-pamby. He has definite understandings about Scripture and about situations in the world. He's very strong inside, but he's also very quiet. His silence does not mean surrender. It speaks more loudly than would his assertiveness. He is a meek man.

All fathers should be meek. Why should they have to bluster and blow and scream and curse to get their way? How much better to be a man who can stand his ground in a nice way. His children and his friends go away from such a father convinced that he is a genuinely good person, a man people enjoy being with.

Do your children say that about you? Do they identify you as a meek person?

**HUNGRY FOR RIGHTEOUSNESS**

Jesus said, *"Blessed are those who hunger and thirst for righteousness, for they shall be satisfied."* "They shall be filled," the King James says.

What do you hunger and thirst for? What did your father before you hunger and thirst for? Of all the qualifications Jesus gives here for a father, I suspect that none has more effect on the overall happiness of the home than this one.

A man who has an earnest desire for goodness is going to bless his family.

Do I need to say that a man who has an earnest desire for badness will curse his family in more ways than we have space to detail? His wrong habits, his ill-turned thoughts, his foolish behavior will afflict everybody who is forced to depend on him.

But a man who desires to be honest, a man who desires to be industrious, a man who desires to be true and pure and good—the kind of man who "hungers and thirsts for righteousness"—will bless all who are part of his life. His goodness bestows order and stability and decency on his family.

I know some people who are good only because they have to be. All of us fit into that category at times, don't we? We're righteous because we don't have any choice. How many of us are good because we want to be? Do we do the right and decent and holy thing because we *want* to?

That's what Jesus is saying here about a father. "Blessed is a father if the desires of his heart have been trained so that what he really wants is the right thing."

## THE MERCIFUL

Then Jesus said, *"Blessed are the merciful, for they shall obtain mercy."* "Mercy" here does not pertain to forgiving. We use the term that way sometimes, but our Lord probably uses the word more broadly.

He alludes here to a special tenderness toward the hurting of others, a quality that is characteristic of God the Father. He knows when we hurt. He knows when we weep. He knows when we feel that our life is boxed in. Our heavenly Father is merciful like that. So should an earthly father be.

Somehow the humanity of our heart has been short-circuited if members of our own family hurt and we do not share their pain. If we feel no need to put an arm around one of our children who is feeling lonely or unloved or confused or bruised, we are lacking in the quality Jesus recommends here.

Especially in their teen years our children get caught in pressures that are incredibly tough for them. They struggle to know who they are, how to get along with their friends, and how to relate to adults, including those in their own family. Awesome biological changes are taking place inside adolescents. It can be a tough time for them, and for family life in general. In these days when our teens almost drive us nuts, how merciful are we to them?

A father who is merciful, Jesus says, will "obtain mercy." Is there a daddy alive who does not need his children to be merciful toward him? Can you exist as a father with children who have grown up to be thirty or forty, and not have those children feel compassionate and understanding toward you?

After preaching a funeral in the Pittsburgh area, I flew home alongside a very sharp Baptist pastor who runs a counseling center. He told me that the number one problem they deal with today are women who come to him in mid-life years to talk of times when their fathers abused them sexually years ago. They pour out all the hate and hurt they feel toward their fathers. Father's Day, he said, is a tough day for women like this, who feel the opposite of mercy for the men who raised them and molested them. Instead, they hate their guts.

## THE PURE IN HEART

*"Blessed are the pure in heart,"* Jesus said, *"for they shall see God."* I don't think he is talking here about morality. That is included in the Beatitude about hungering for righteousness. Saying you are "pure in heart" is about the same thing a milk producer says when he labels his carton "100% pure milk." This is all one thing. This is undiluted. It's not a mixture. It's the genuine item.

"Blessed are the pure in heart" describes the single-minded person who has set his mind totally to do what he's going to do in life. He has devoted himself to Christ and to the church and to the good of his family. He has his priorities lined up right. He is goal-oriented toward things that matter for him and his.

What a blessing for a family to have a daddy who knows what he must be doing!

One day in DFW airport I ran into my friend Jim Shewmaker. He's always such an upbeat guy. I love to visit with him. At some point in our discussion that day, we got onto the subject of people's attitudes toward church. Jim said, "Ten years ago when I went to the church we belong to, I made a commitment in my mind. 'We will give this congregation ten years of our lives, regardless. I will be here that long whether the preacher does good work or not, whether the money comes in or not, whether the church is prospering or declining. I will be here at least ten years.'"

Jim smiled and said, "You know, that turned my life loose. Our church has gone through some hard times, but I don't have to get up every morning and wonder if I should be a part of it. I committed my life to that effort, and I will be there, regardless." That is pureness of heart.

A man who is pure in heart says, "I am married. I intend to stay married. There may be days when I want to kill her—we may have times when the relationship is stormy or cold or nasty—but I will stick it out. The bills may be too high sometimes and the kids may be bad, but I will be the father of my family regardless."

When a man sets that sort of goal without allowing other options to mislead him from his responsibilities, he is pure in heart in the way Jesus uses the term in this Beatitude. That would bless any family, wouldn't it?

## THE PEACEMAKERS

*"Blessed are the peacemakers."*

Do I need to write anything about this one?

Some of us, wherever we go, stir up trouble. Some of us, wherever we go, put oil on the water.

A father who causes his kids to talk nice to one another just because he is there, the daddy who just because he is there dispels jealousy and envy between his kids and makes them love one another—such a father has really blessed his home. He is a peacemaker, and according to Jesus, he will be called a child of God.

## THE PERSECUTED

*"Blessed are those who are persecuted for righteousness' sake, for theirs is the kingdom of heaven."*

In this Beatitude Jesus gives us a description of commitment to right behavior, a commitment that does not bend or dissolve under pressure. Some men intend to be good, but they intend rather feebly. They really mean to do better than they do on the job, but along comes a temptation they do not anticipate, and they crumble. They have no backbone for goodness.

A father who is willing to suffer, to be persecuted, "for righteousness' sake" is a rare individual. In such a man there is a strength of faith and commitment that inspires respect for him from his family and his friends. His children look back later and say, "I had a father who had real principles." They probably don't always agree with him. Not if they are normal kids. But they still have a deep-down respect for him because they know he will do what is right regardless of any sort of pressure that may come along.

Jesus expands this idea when he talks about the blessedness that belongs to a person whose enemies utter all kinds of evil against him falsely for His account. You are blessed, Jesus says, if people are saying all sorts of nasty things about you not just because you are good but because you are a Christian.

A daddy like that really blesses a family. He has a commitment to the Lord and to the church and to the faith that cannot be shaken by mistreatment or hardship. Such a father should "rejoice and be glad," Jesus says, for his reward "is great in heaven."

**THE BEST BLESSINGS**

When we look at the Beatitudes in the light I have just suggested, and then go back and look at the blessings attached to each of them, it amazes us to see what can happen to the individual who conforms his life to these standards.

What does Jesus say about a father who lives like this?

He will possess the Kingdom.
He will be comforted.
He will inherit the earth.
He will be satisfied or filled.
He will obtain mercy.
He will see God.
He will be called a child of God.
Great rewards in heaven will belong to him.

These blessings will belong to a man whose life measures up to Jesus' standards in these short verses.

These are the promises of the Beatitudes. Any father who lives like this will be richly fulfilled, satisfied, and happy.

This is the sort of father Jesus wants every man to be.

**CHAPTER TWO**

# SALT AND LIGHT

*You are the salt of the earth; but if salt has lost its taste, how shall its saltness be restored? It is no longer good for anything except to be thrown out and trodden under foot by men.*

*You are the light of the world. A city set on a hill cannot be hid. Nor do men light a lamp and put it under a bushel, but on a stand, and it gives light to all in the house. Let your light so shine before men, that they may see your good works and give glory to your Father who is in heaven* (Matthew 5:13-16).

Jesus tells his followers, "You are the salt of the earth. You are the light of the world."

I wonder. In our home life these days do those of us who wear Jesus' name qualify for such a lofty description? Are we really the salt of the earth, the light of the world?

When people look at our homes, do they see a better quality of life than they see in other homes around us?

Does believing in Christ make me a more loving father than if I did not believe in him?

Does confessing Jesus make you a wiser mother?

Does your Christian faith make you a more obedient son or daughter?

Is your home happier, calmer, stabler because you are a Christian?

Is your marriage more likely to hang together because you follow Jesus?

How would your family's leisure activities change if you were not a Christian?

Is the neighborhood you live in more desirable because yours is a Christian family, or would some of the neighbors sigh with relief if you moved out?

If we are serious at all about Jesus' teaching that we are the salt of the earth and the light of the world, we need to ask ourselves questions like these.

In what sense do we live up to our Lord's intention that our families be the salt and the light in our culture?

## HOMES THAT LAST

Do our kids really behave better than the kids across the street who never see the inside of a church building?

Are our teenagers less likely than the pagan neighbors to come home drunk or high on Saturday night?

Will our young people do better in school? Will they have fewer scrapes with the law? And will they show more respect for adults because they belong to Christian families? Or will the church have to hide her face because of our adolescents' unruly antics?

Are the people at school delighted to know that another student from your church is enrolling? Or do they groan?

## BLACK EYES

I have served in local church ministry for more than forty years. Part of the pleasure of those years has been working with top-notch families who have done a good job raising their kids. I would agree with Jesus that most of the Christian families I have known have been exemplary. Their lifestyle and their values have set them apart as special people in a muddled, mixed-up world. They truly have been salt and light, and I have been proud to speak up and say, "Yes, those are our people. They serve the Lord in our congregation. Aren't they fine?"

But this has not always been true. Can you imagine the chagrin I felt when the foster care officials in Arizona called me years ago and said, "We would like for you to be present for a custody hearing Friday morning." In my youthful naïveté I was shocked to hear that one of our strictest members had been sexually abusing his teenage daughter, and the state was taking steps to remove her from her Christian home.

What could I say to the welfare worker who called me? I was heartbroken and ashamed. "Let none of you suffer as a murderer, or as a thief, or as a wrongdoer, or as a mischief-maker," Peter commands the church (1 Peter 4:15). But right in our fellowship, masquerading as the truest of the true and often vocal in condemning others, was a father guilty of the sort of immorality that outrages even the pagans around us. His behavior was now a matter of public record. He gave our faith a black eye.

So did the sweet little Christian girl in another church I served. She turned up with syphilis at 14 and, according to the public health people, could not determine which of several partners might have given it to her. She also gave the church a black eye.

So did the Christian woman who beat up her husband and intimidated him so badly he had to call the police to protect him while he retrieved his clothes from his own house.

So did the man who sat in our pews and played "Mr. O.K." every Sunday until one day the sheriff showed up at the large store where he worked and hauled him off to jail for the hot checks he had spread all over the county he had just moved from.

So did the teenager who came to church with his family every Sunday, and served the Lord's Supper on some of those Sundays, after being hauled home by his buddies almost every Saturday night so drunk he could not find his own front door.

So did two of our former deacons who cheated on their wives and bragged about it to their non-church associates.

These people gave the church a black eye in our community. They were *not* the salt of the earth. They were *not* the light of the world. They were a disgrace to the name of Jesus.

Every one of them had been baptized in Jesus' name. I had personally baptized some of them. All of them had confessed the name of Jesus before their family and friends. But later they denied him by the way they lived.

I am convinced that no such thing exists as a "victimless crime" or a "private sin." "What I do is my own business," misbehaving grown-up children often blurt out to distance their inquiring parents. "How I conduct my life is of no concern to you," sinning church members sometimes reply to church leaders concerned about their life-ruining immoralities. But the children and the church members asserting their moral independence are wrong. Every sin we commit tarnishes the reputation of the church and wounds the hearts of those we love.

## PROMPTING PRAISE

The sad examples I have just cited brought shame on the church and caused outsiders to criticize the church. In the Sermon on the Mount Jesus calls us to grow families and lifestyles that will draw exactly the opposite response. He wants people around us to see "our good works," and he says the result should be that they "give glory to our Father who is in heaven."

From its earliest days Christianity has always been "on display." Critics of the faith, and those who just wonder about it, have watched Christians to see if following Jesus makes any real difference in the quality of their lives. The main observation window has always been the home.

Consider the ministry of Titus, for example.

On the island of Crete, the young minister Titus faced the awesome task of instructing a church full of brand-new converts who had grown up in the moral armpit of the pagan world. Even their own poets described the Cretan people as "always liars, evil beasts, and lazy gluttons."

In this tough setting Titus learned the urgency of Jesus' call for his followers to be salt and light in the world. Paul knew that opponents of Christianity would be scrutinizing those new Christians, looking for the smallest flaw. Home life would be the first place the critics looked for Christianity to fail. So Paul cautioned the young preacher to shape his people up in this area. In Titus 2 the apostle gave specific instructions for the families in that church.

The old men—the grandfathers of the families—needed to be "temperate, serious, sensible, sound in faith, in love, and in steadfastness," Paul told Titus. Ancient cultures looked respectfully to the elderly for wisdom and guidance. If the elders in the Christian community turned out to be silly old men who wasted their days in drunkenness and empty palavering, the church would quickly lose all respect in that society.

On the shoulders of the older women fell the heaviest responsibility for establishing showcase homes in the church. "They are to teach what is good," Paul said, "and so train the young women to love their husbands and children, to be sensible, chaste, domestic, kind, and submissive to their husbands."

What does it mean to be "domestic"? The King James Version translates this "keepers at home." Did Paul mean by this that a young mother could never leave her house? Surely not. But he certainly was saying that caring for the home is a high priority item for a Christian wife.

Don't misunderstand me. I am not suggesting that it is wrong for a Christian mother to be employed. But surely you will agree that if a modern lady snags a vice-presidency in a prestigious firm while her home is in shambles and her children grow up un-mothered and neglected, we could not describe such a woman as "domestic," could we?

How effectively do the older women in today's churches teach younger Christian women to be "chaste"? I cannot think of anything more important to teach in a world where all marriages—Christian and otherwise—are threatened by a growing moral laxity. We have failed our young women in the church if we let them grow up without learning how to be friendly without being flirty.

Is it the church's job to teach young mothers how to keep house, how to budget family finances, or how to care for their children? Titus 2:4-5 seems to imply that. Paul says Christian wives and mothers must be good at what they do for an important reason: *"that the word of God may not be discredited."*

## MASCULINE MATTERS

Of course the task of forging a Christian home is not the work of a woman alone. Husbands and fathers are charged by God with heavy responsibility in this area. Paul covered an incredibly broad spectrum of behavior when he told Titus, "Urge the younger men to control themselves." So much of the havoc I have seen in failing homes can be traced to a lack of discipline and control.

One young couple I counseled seemed surprised to learn that they were spending three times their monthly income every month. Unchecked spending wrecked their marriage. Uncontrolled lusts ruin others. Lack of discipline in work habits can bring any home to its knees. A man whose unbridled temper makes him unable to hold a job will be a curse to his home. A Christian man who dares to abuse his wife or his children brings untold agony to his family and unthinkable shame to the church.

"Urge the young men to control themselves." Paul could not have offered more practical advice for strengthening Christian homes and for making them a credit to the Lord we serve. Husbands who always behave leave the enemy "nothing evil to say of us," Paul pointed out. When we live upright, godly, sensible lives in our homes, Paul told Titus, "we adorn the doctrine of God our Savior."

## A WAY TO PREACH

Did you ever wish you could preach? You can. And you don't have to climb into a pulpit to do it. "You are the light of the world," Jesus said, and if you help your family to put together an exemplary Christian home, your light "cannot be hid."

The "doctrine of God our Savior" is adorned and validated to your friends when they see that believing in Jesus has made your home what they would like for theirs to be.

Back in the early 1960's, a team of my classmates from Abilene Christian University went as missionaries to Brazil. They took with them movie projectors and powerful films, printing presses and well-planned teaching. All of these tools helped them to evangelize, but they were surprised to find that their strongest presentation of the Christian gospel turned out to be their own Christian marriages.

In that culture the prevailing religion winked at a husband's extramarital sexual activities. The local women were amazed to find that the missionaries' wives trusted their husbands to be true to them. "Is this for real?" they asked in amazement. When they observed the missionaries' home life, these women decided that they, too, would like to profess a faith that would make their husbands faithful.

What about your marriage, your home? Are you the salt of the earth and the light of the world as Jesus means for you to be?

Will people want to share your faith because of the things that happen where you live?

CHAPTER THREE

# DOING WHAT GOD WANTS US TO

*Think not that I have come to abolish the law and the prophets; I have come not to abolish them but to fulfil them. For truly, I say to you, till heaven and earth pass away, not an iota, not a dot, will pass from the law until all is accomplished. Whoever then relaxes one of the least of these commandments and teaches men so, shall be called least in the kingdom of heaven; but he who does them and teaches them shall be called great in the kingdom of heaven. For I tell you, unless your righteousness exceeds that of the scribes and Pharisees, you will never enter the kingdom of heaven.*

*You have heard that it was said to the men of old, "You shall not kill; and whoever kills shall be liable to judgment." But I say to you that every one who is angry with his brother shall be liable to judgment; whoever insults his brother shall be liable to the council, and whoever says, "You fool!" shall be liable to the hell of fire. So if you are offering your gift at the altar, and there remember that your brother has something against you, leave your gift there before the altar and go; first be reconciled to your brother, and then come and offer your gift. Make friends quickly with your accuser, while you are going with him to court, lest your accuser hand you over to the judge, and the judge to the guard, and you be put in prison; truly, I say to you, you will never get out till you have paid the last penny.*

*You have heard that it was said, "You shall not commit adultery." But I say to you that every one who looks at a woman lustfully has already committed adultery with her in his heart. If your right eye causes you to sin, pluck it out and throw it away; it is better that you lose one of your members than that your whole body be thrown into hell. And if your right hand causes you to sin, cut it off and throw it away; it is better that you lose one of your members than that your whole body go into hell.*

*It was also said, "Whoever divorces his wife, let him give her a certificate of divorce." But I say to you that every one who divorces his wife, except on the ground of unchastity, makes her an adulteress; and whoever marries a divorced woman commits adultery.*

*Again you have heard that it was said to the men of old, "You shall not swear falsely, but shall perform to the Lord what you have sworn." But I say to you, Do not swear at all, either by heaven, for it is the throne of God, or by the earth, for it is his footstool, or by Jerusalem, for it is the city of the great King. And do not swear by your head, for you cannot make one hair white or black. Let what you say be simply "Yes" or "No"; anything more than this comes from evil.*

*You have heard that it was said, "An eye for an eye and a tooth for a tooth." But I say to you, Do not resist one who is evil. But if any one strikes you on the right cheek, turn to him the other also; and if any one would sue you and take your coat, let him have your cloak as well; and if any one forces you to go one mile, go with him two miles. Give to him who begs from you, and do not refuse him who would borrow from you.*

*You have heard that it was said, "You shall love your neighbor and hate your enemy." But I say to you, Love your enemies and pray for those who persecute you, so that you may be sons of your Father who is in heaven; for he makes his sun rise on the evil and on the good, and sends rain on the just and on the unjust. For if you love those who love you, what reward have you? Do not even the tax collectors do the same? And if you salute only your brethren, what more are you doing than others? Do not even the Gentiles do the same? You, therefore, must be perfect, as your heavenly Father is perfect* (Matthew 5:17-48).

People have always found it easier to keep the rules of religion than to do what God really wants us to do.

That is what Jesus is telling us in this part of Matthew 5. Like waves breaking one after the other on the seashore, the familiar phrases of Jesus assail our minds over and over and over again.

*"You have heard that it was said to the men of old. . . . But I say to you."*

*"You have heard that it was said. . . . But I say to you."*

Again and again in the Sermon on the Mount Jesus repeats those phrases. Not once, not twice, but six times our Lord poses the conflict.

"Here is what you have been taught by the interpreters of God's law. Here is what *I* say to you about it."

"Here is the commonly accepted understanding of God's law on this matter. Here is *my* explanation of what God really intended."

Thus, with bulldog tenacity, Jesus hammered home his call for a brand of righteousness almost unknown even to the most religious people of his day. "Unless your righteousness exceeds that of the scribes and Pharisees," he told his hearers, "you will never enter the kingdom of heaven."

The scribes and Pharisees thought they were the finest folks around, but Jesus said his followers would have to be better than those religious perfectionists just to get inside the front door of his Kingdom. Had Jesus been preaching today, he probably would have said, "Except your righteousness exceeds that of the church folks in town, you'll never get into the Kingdom."

## THE WRONG KIND OF RIGHTNESS

What was wrong with the righteousness of the scribes and Pharisees?

We need to know. If we're going to apply this important teaching of Jesus to our families and homes, we need to know what sort of righteousness pleases the Lord and what sort falls short of his standards. We need to avoid the wrong kind of righteousness and opt for the right kind.

Some families I know about may help us understand what Jesus has in mind.

I am thinking, for example, about a father who insisted on daily family devotionals in his home. Not a day could be missed. But the same man went into furious tirades because his neighbor on the south let dandelions bloom and blow into his yard.

Another man I know was outspokenly proud that he read through his Bible from cover to cover every year. But the same fellow "overlooked" paying the Christian mechanic and the Christian grocer who extended credit to his family.

One prominent family in our town seldom misses a service at their church, but they agreed together last winter to call in "sick" at school so their kids could go skiing.

I'm not talking here about bad people. The people in these families are openly religious people who are making an effort to live up to the rules and regulations of their churches. They are not rowdy galoots tearing up town in drunk-and-disorderly mayhem, nor are they pseudo-sophisticates who selfishly pursue unnatural sex and thus infect their world with a deadly plague. For the most part the people I have just described are decent, moral, honest, dependable, church-going folks, but in their homes they have not found the kind of righteousness Jesus calls us to.

Rule-keeping righteousness always falls short of Christ's standard. *We can keep all the rules and still not do what God wants us to.*

"You shall not murder" is an important rule for human conduct. Even the pagans among us recognize that. My neighbors who never go to church would never dream of breaking this rule. Not for one minute have I ever worried about one of them murdering me.

But Jesus wants us to know that when God said, "Thou shalt not kill," he had a great deal more in mind than just preserving human life. He wanted to curtail the hatred and hostility that turn men into murderers. He meant to outlaw the jealousy and anger that cause a man like Cain to bash in the brains of his brother.

If I never lay violent hands on another human being but spend most of my adult life seething with resentment toward one of my own bloodkin, I have kept God's rule and still have done the opposite of what he wants me to do.

This is what Jesus is saying to us in Matthew 5.

## GOOD ON THE INSIDE

"You shall not commit adultery," is the second God-given rule Jesus cites to illustrate his point. Unfortunately this rule has lost much of its punch in our sex-mad society. Murder is still an unthinkable offense in polite society. We would never decide to keep quiet and look the other way while a known murderer masqueraded as a corporate executive or a prominent lawyer or a top surgeon in our town, but today flagrant adulterers occupy positions of trust, and we say nothing.

More than half a million teen abortions in America last year bear witness that our nation is doing a poor job of keeping God's rule for sex. In

1970, only 1 American adolescent in 47 was infected with a sexually transmitted disease. Today the infection rate for teens is 1 in 4. More than 1.3 million babies born last year to unwed mothers and over 15 million new cases of sexually transmitted diseases every year in America sadly indicate that we are not paying much attention to the Seventh Commandment.

But the rule is not completely extinct. Bill Clinton and Gary Condit and Jim Bakker can assure us of that. On some levels of society, at least, we still expect people to save sex for the marriage bed. In the church especially we have maintained high standards for sexual behavior. Few churches would knowingly ordain an active adulterer as an elder or a deacon or a minister. We expect Christians to keep this rule.

Jesus wants us to know, however, that we can keep the rule strictly and still violate most of what God intended when he wrote on Mount Sinai, "Thou shalt not commit adultery." The man who burns with desire for his stepdaughter, or his sister-in-law, or his niece is being driven from within by an unrighteousness that flies in the face of God's will. Although he never touches the forbidden woman, although he perfectly keeps the rule against adultery, still if his heart is ravaged by an unholy lust, he is violating God's intent. On the outside he keeps God's rule. On the inside he is exactly what God does not want him to be.

## GOD'S LAW AND US

Most of the teaching I have heard about this section of the Sermon on the Mount dealt with the relationship between Jesus' teaching and Moses' law. Ever since the early 1800s when Alexander Campbell preached his famous sermon on the Law and the Gospel, the churches I grew up in have been fascinated as a people with the end of the Old Covenant and the beginning of the New. As good theological lawyers, our preachers and teachers over the past century and a half have constructed elaborate doctrinal schemes based on these distinctions.

Not for a moment do I doubt that Jesus sealed a New Covenant with his blood. He said he did. Nor do I doubt that Jesus nailed the Old Law to the cross. The apostles said he did. I believe all that. But I don't think this is the truth Jesus has in mind in the last half of Matthew 5. In this great sermon our Lord is talking not so much about *his* relationship to the Law as he is talking about *our* relationship to it.

Are we just keeping the outward rules, Jesus wants to know, or are we really living the intent of God's laws? That is the thrust of Matthew 5. Christ's teaching here is not just an upgrade of Moses. It is an explanation of Moses. It's not enough just to keep the rules, Jesus insists. Are we doing what God wants us to?

**CLOSER TO HOME**

Now let's bring Jesus' truth closer to home. In fact, let's apply it to our own homes. As the words of the Sermon on the Mount zoom in on our families, let's allow our Lord's high standards of righteousness and his probing truths to measure the quality of goodness in our lives and our homes.

Hear Jesus as he asks, "You who are so religious, are you really doing what God wants you to in your homes?"

How nearly, for example, are we obeying God's will about divorce? This is what Jesus wants to know in verses 31 and 32. Religious rules about divorce are not nearly so stiff in America today as they were just a few decades ago. Divorces once were rare in Christian circles. Today the rarity is the family in the church who can say they are untouched by divorce. Hardly a month passes without some family in the church calling to tell me that one of their kids or grandkids is getting a divorce. It makes me want to weep.

While we remain convinced that God's grace applies to the sin of divorce the same as to any other sin, we must confess that the frequency of divorce in Christian families is alarming. In a single year a few decades ago this sin alone devastated my own congregation.

The fact that most of our congregations are trying to be more gracious and less condemning toward divorced people should not lull us into thinking that divorce has somehow become an O.K. option for solving our minor marital messes. In Matthew 5:31-32 the Lord sets forth his will for our marriages quite plainly. He wants our marriages to last.

In our families, are we doing what God wants us to do about divorce?

## NOTHING BUT THE TRUTH

If divorce is a touchy topic, the next area Jesus probes in his sermon is even more so. Do we always tell the truth? Can people depend on what we tell them? All the time? Without fail?

As a child I heard many discussions among leaders of the church about whether it was proper for a Christian to sign an oath of allegiance to the government in order to take a federal job, or whether a Christian could swear in court to tell "the truth, the whole truth, and nothing but the truth, so help me God."

Of course, those church leaders were concerned about Jesus' remarks in this section of Matthew 5. "Do not swear at all," Jesus says, and those good men took him quite literally, failing to see that our Lord was addressing a use of oaths not even remotely connected to the kind they were worried about.

In their perplexity about swearing legally on behalf of Uncle Sam, those church leaders seldom got around to hearing what Jesus is really telling us. "Tell the truth all the time" is not too lax a paraphrase of our Lord's instructions here. We don't need a string of fancy superlatives or elaborate oaths to add verity to our words. If we always tell the truth, a simple Yes or No will suffice to make others believe us.

How closely does this description fit the language in our homes?

I still remember my mother's gentle reproof when I began to embellish my 10-year-old conversations by exclaiming, "Well, I'll be a monkey's uncle!"

She wisely advised me that I was spouting empty words I did not really mean, and she reminded me of Jesus' requirement that our language be simple, direct, and true.

## COATS AND CLOAKS

Is anything Jesus taught any harder for us to live up to than his requirement that we not resist evil people and that we love our enemies?

The religious rules in Jesus' day allowed people personally to avenge any wrong done to them. Their only limitation was what lawyers today call "proportionality"—the nature of the vengeance had to fit the nature of the crime. "An eye for an eye, and a tooth for a tooth" was the

Bible rule of fairness and temperance in response to offenses. You couldn't kill a man for stealing a chicken, and you couldn't cut off his hand for stealing a loaf of bread.

This rule, intended by God to soften angry reprisals against those who wronged others, was twisted by the religious teachers of Jesus' time to mean that vengeance must always be inflicted on one who did wrong. "An eye for an eye" became not a modifier of vengeance but a mandate for it. Jesus teaches us that this is exactly the opposite of what God intends. "I say to you, Do not resist one who is evil. But if anyone strikes you on the right cheek, turn to him the other also."

How do you handle offenses in your home?

If your wife ticks you off, does she get the silent treatment for the next three days?

If your husband slights you, is the bed off-limits until you get over being mad?

If one of your in-laws does you dirty, do you write that person out of your life for the rest of your days?

How do you respond in your family to those who wrong you?

Are anger and resentment a daily diet at your table? Is someone in your home continually talking about how miffed he or she is at somebody at work or at church?

Or have you learned to react to offenses as Jesus teaches—by praying for your enemies and by repaying mistreatment with acts of kindness? In circumstances like these, have you learned to do what God wants you to?

**CHILDREN OF THE FATHER**

Are you a child of God? At the conclusion of this section of Jesus' sermon, he zeroes in on this question.

God's children are like him, Jesus says. They don't just wear the label "children of God." They behave as God would behave in the same circumstances. They do what God would do.

We need to pray for our enemies, Jesus tells us, *"so that you may be sons of your Father who is in heaven."* We may go to the right church, believe all the right doctrines, submit to all the right rituals—in other words, we can keep all the rules of religion—and still not be children of God unless we choose to be like him.

God forgives those who do wrong. He makes his sun shine every morning even on those who are bad. He causes the rain to fall even on the unjust. If we're going to be children of God, Jesus insists, we've got to act like God. "You, therefore, must be perfect, as your heavenly Father is perfect."

That's a large order, but isn't that the goal of all valid faith—to become like God?

If we approach religion as rulekeepers, our goal so often is merely to justify ourselves and to legalize our misbehavior. But a person who truly trusts in God and lives for him wants more than anything else in this world to become like him.

**CHAPTER FOUR**

# THE REWARDS OF WORSHIP

*Beware of practicing your piety before men in order to be seen by them; for then you will have no reward from your Father who is in heaven.*

*Thus, when you give alms, sound no trumpet before you, as the hypocrites do in the synagogues and in the streets, that they may be praised by men. Truly, I say to you, they have received their reward. But when you give alms, do not let your left hand know what your right hand is doing, so that your alms may be in secret; and your Father who sees in secret will reward you.*

*And when you pray, you must not be like the hypocrites; for they love to stand and pray in the synagogues and at the street corners, that they may be seen by men. Truly, I say to you, they have received their reward. But when you pray, go into your room and shut the door and pray to your Father who is in secret; and your Father who sees in secret will reward you.*

*And in praying do not heap up empty phrases as the Gentiles do; for they think that they will be heard for their many words. Do not be like them, for your Father knows what you need before you ask him. Pray then like this:*

*Our Father who art in heaven,*
*Hallowed be thy name.*
*Thy kingdom come.*
*Thy will be done,*
*On earth as it is in heaven.*
*Give us this day our daily bread;*
*And forgive us our debts,*
*As we also have forgiven our debtors;*
*And lead us not into temptation,*
*But deliver us from evil.*

*For if you forgive men their trespasses, your heavenly Father also will forgive you; but if you do not forgive men their trespasses, neither will your Father forgive your trespasses.*

*And when you fast, do not look dismal, like the hypocrites, for they disfigure their faces that their fasting may be seen by men. Truly, I say to you, they have received their reward. But when you fast, anoint your head and wash your face, that your fasting may not be seen by men but by your Father who is in secret; and your Father who sees in secret will reward you* (Matthew 6:1-18).

Few of us are familiar with the name of Taras Shevchenko. But if we lived in the Soviet Union in the Ukraine, where my missionary friend Stephan Bilak grew up, we would know the name and the fame of Shevchenko.

A poet and a painter who died just before America's Civil War, Shevchenko spoke out for undenominational Christianity in the Ukraine. Because of his dedication and his fearless proclamation of the gospel, he is still credited by many of his countrymen with saving the faith of his people.

I tell you about this remarkable Soviet believer in order to share with you one line he wrote. "My greatest delight in life," he said, "is reading the New Testament daily."

As we continue to search in the Sermon on the Mount for Jesus' message to our families, let me borrow Shevchenko's line to help us check up on our devotion to Christ.

If you are a mother, for example, how would you complete that old Russian's sentence, "My greatest delight in life is . . ."? Would you say, "My greatest delight in life is . . .

—getting to watch two hours of TV without the kids having a fight?

—watching my child hit a homerun?

—making it through a month without a doctor bill?

—getting to sleep in and not go to work on a holiday?

If you're a father, how would you finish the sentence? Would you say, "My greatest delight in life is . . .

—finally getting to buy a new car?

—finding a whole day free to play golf (or to fish, or to hunt)?

—getting a promotion or a raise?

—going camping with my wife and my kids?

Kids, it's your turn now. What pleases you most in life? Would you say, "My greatest delight in life is. . .

—getting a date with the "right" person at school?

—getting a date? Period.

—getting a driver's license and my own set of wheels?

—getting to goof off with my friends?

I don't know what delights you the most in life, but I suspect that most of us have no trouble seeing the gap between our values and those of Taras Shevchenko. Here was a man who said unashamedly that the activity which pleased him more than any other in the world was *getting to read the New Testament daily.*

Shevchenko was a man whose God mattered more to him than anything else that touched his life.

**WHO OR WHAT WE LOVE**

What about us? What takes first place in our lives?

When Jesus gives instructions for worship at the beginning of Matthew 6, this is his main concern. His real subject is not *how* we worship; his real concern is *who* we worship.

"Set your affections on things that are above, not on things that are on the earth," Paul taught his converts. He realized that all of us are being tugged and torn from opposite directions. All of us are feeling attractions from above and from below, from the holy and from the unholy.

"No man can serve two masters," Jesus will say in the next few verses of the Sermon on the Mount. The competition for our souls never stops.

But our Lord may have put it most simply in these early verses of Matthew 6. These eighteen verses of Scripture boil down to one plain question: *Do we love us more than we love God?*

One answer to the question, Jesus says, is revealed in our worship.

Do we perform the rituals of our faith because we adore God, or because we want people to adore us? Do we offer lavish gifts to God because we want to honor him, or because we want other people to honor us?

Are our prayers a pure expression of our desire to glorify the Lord, or do they somehow turn out to be a "holy" way for us to seek glory for ourselves?

Jesus' teaching strikes at the very root of who we are and why we are involved in this thing called religion. Christ is a bit sneaky here. To speak to an age which has decided to "serve the creature rather than the Creator," our Lord slips up on us by talking about the seemingly safe act of worship, but he's really challenging us to look honestly at ourselves.

When we do pause and reflect, in response to Jesus' words, it should be clear to us that if we praise God to make other people praise us, we aren't really praising God at all. Hymns sung to impress others bring glory only to us, not to him. Sermons preached to demonstrate the brilliance of the preacher do not cause the Lord to shine before men.

We detract from the glory that belongs to God whenever we do anything in worship for the purpose of making people praise us.

## "SEEN BY MEN"

When Nita and I were raising our kids, we never made it a practice to say grace in a restaurant before we ate. Somehow it seemed pretentious for us to bow our heads in a public place before God-only-knows-how-many pagans to say our private family prayers. We always thanked God for our food at our home table, of course, but café-praying was not our bag. From time to time, though, we go out to eat with Christian friends who want to pray over their food—regardless of the location, so we get trapped into praying with them at a café table. I'm always uncomfortable doing it. I feel entirely too much like the hypocrites Jesus criticized for standing on the street corners and praying "that they may be seen of men."

Don't misunderstand. I don't mention this in order to criticize those of you who may be café-pray-ers. My purpose is to try to clarify Jesus' teaching here. Perhaps I should hasten to tell you that two of my own fleshly brothers disagree with me on this. They insist on praying in cafés. They argue, not without merit, that Christians should not be ashamed of their devotion to God. Prayers before meals, they say, are one of the customs our culture identifies as "Christian," so nobody should be offended if we bow our heads before we eat our eggs at Denny's. Any onlookers might think we are denying our faith if we don't say grace, and Jesus did warn us that if we're ashamed of him before other people, he will deny us before the Father, didn't he? This, my café-praying brothers contend, is a silent, unobtrusive way for us to confess our Lord and our faith.

All of this may be true, and my brothers are likely more righteous than I, but I'm still uncomfortable about parading my prayers in public places—especially if I am doing it with the express purpose of trying to impress others with the intensity of my Christian devotion. That seems to be precisely the sort of thing Jesus tells us not to do.

Anything I do in worship to call attention to me is somehow tainted. Whether I am preaching or praying or wearing my new Easter frock in the third pew, it seems to me that I am violating Jesus' plain teaching if my primary intent during a time of public worship is to make people admire me. Pure and holy worship is designed to make people admire God.

"Not to us, O Lord, not to us, but to thy name give glory," the Psalmist taught us to pray (115:1). Can you think of a better motto for worship?

**HEART TESTS**

So Jesus calls us into the sanctuary—into the place of worship—to test our hearts. Here, where our very presence seems to speak of faith and trust and belief and humility and devotion—here, where all our words and acts are supposedly expressions of love for our Maker—here Jesus bids us examine our worship to find out if we really love God more than we love ourselves.

Isn't it amazing how simply and how subtly our acts of worship betray who we really are? And who we really love?

If I love me more than God, my chief concern in giving at church is to be sure that somebody—hopefully a lot of somebodies—will know how generous I am. If I can't give without blowing a trumpet to gather an audience, is there any doubt about my main motive for the donation?

If I love me more than God, my public prayers are likely to be longer than normal, more eloquent than normal. I will do *something* when I pray to call attention to me—if I love God less than I love me.

I was troubled several years ago when I attended a church where the song leader put on a circus performance. Nobody in the assembly that morning had their minds on the Lord we were singing about. Jesus got up-staged that day by the song leader. I don't think many of us were praising the song leader either (although he obviously was laboring mightily to evoke our praise). Most of us fervently wished he would just vanish and let someone else lead us in unpretentious praise to God.

Perhaps we should quickly confess that the ego which made that little man ruin our worship that day can be found in all of us, and we don't have to go to church to practice it. Jesus identified worship as one arena where self-love becomes stinkingly, sickeningly visible, but the sinful self in each of us constantly strives in every part of life to take God's place and to soak up all the praise and devotion and attention due only to the Almighty.

How many of us in today's world, for example, put God first when we plan the use of our time? Are we not prone to program our weeks with multiple hours for amusement and playtime for all of our pet projects and our extra jobs—with relatively few minutes left over for cultivating the Spirit and contemplating Christ and serving his people? Whole weeks pass for some of us without a single church service attended or a single Bible verse read. Instead, all the time has been spent on ourselves. When this happens, it is plain to us and to God who we love best.

What percentage of your family budget does God get? If the church received the same amount you spend each year to vacation and play, how much would your giving increase? How much could the mission and benevolent works of the church expand? Satan would like to convince us that we "deserve" all the luxuries and trinkets and trips we fritter away our money on. He is delighted when we worship one hour a week and give God twenty bucks out of a thousand, and then spend all the rest of our time and money on ourselves.

I realize that deciding what portion of our day or our dollar belongs to God may not be as simple as it sounds at first. The main service some of us offer to God may be the work we do for a living. That is where we touch lives with the gifts God has given us. That is where we extend his love to people who sorely need it. And the hours we spend playing may be spent precisely to regroup our strength and to find fresh energy to do the things God calls us to do for him. Likewise, the dollars we invest in what may appear to be frivolous to some folks may really be part of our total plan for a life devoted to the Almighty. The important test in all of this is whether or not our most basic intent is to honor him with our lives and our possessions. If God is first in our lives—all the time—these matters take care of themselves.

That's the question: Is he first? Sometimes when God sees our choices, he must feel like the anxious girl who plucks the daisy's petals and says, "He loves me. He loves me not. He loves me. . . ."

"You shall love the Lord your God with *all* your heart," Jesus tells us. This is the very first—the most important—of all the commandments, he insists. All the rituals we perform, all the doctrines we believe, all the scriptures we memorize, and all the prayers we recite amount to nothing if we distort this first commandment so that we love *ourselves* with all our hearts.

### REAL WORSHIP

Dr. Warren Wiersbe wrote a power-packed little book entitled *Real Worship.* Twice in the early pages of the book he warns, "If you worship because it pays, it won't pay."

That's another way of saying what Jesus tells us in Matthew 6. If we worship to praise God in heaven, *he* rewards us. *He* pays. But if we worship only to make the people around us think we're neat, they probably will. But God won't.

From heaven there is no reward for self-worship. If we are seeking earthly benefits from our acts of praise, that is all we're apt to get. As Jesus says, we have our reward, and it is a puny one indeed.

Once every year I compile a list of those who have given money during the past twelve months to help us publish my devotional magazine *The Christian Appeal.* This week I have been working on that list again. Almost every year we have some donors who have given large contributions who ask to remain anonymous. I think I know why. They have read what Jesus says in Matthew 6, and they want to give in secret so that "the Father who sees in secret" may reward them. They want God's favor, not yours and mine.

Of course, we do not publish the list of *Christian Appeal* donors to give honor or praise to any person. Our only purpose is to be accountable to our supporters—to let them know exactly where our money comes from, where it goes, and how much it takes to accomplish this ministry for the Lord. We don't think that publishing these names violates our Lord's teaching about secrecy in giving. His emphasis seems to be not so much on secrecy as on our unholy desire to let our gifts be seen by others.

I do not mean to throw rocks at any good work, but I strongly believe that we who are called upon to contribute to Christian works need to be cautious about any fund-raising efforts which attempt to get our money by offering to honor us. Such fund-raising violates what Jesus teaches us about "practicing our piety before men," because it tempts us to seek honor for ourselves instead of giving it to the Lord. All of us who raise money for Christian ministries owe it to our Lord and to our contributors not to appeal to this carnal motive. Satan's temptations in this area are strong enough without Christians adding to them.

## WHERE CHRIST COMES FIRST

Let me encourage you to sit down in your home and talk candidly as a family about *why* you worship and about *who* you worship. If it's just you and your spouse now, or if you still have kids at home, sit down with your family group, read the first eighteen verses of Matthew 6, and do some soul-searching based on Jesus' instructions here.

Ask, for example: How much of our family's worship arises from a pure love for God? How much of it stems from the expectation of grandparents or in-laws or other relatives?

Ask each family member to reflect on whether they come to worship because of their own personal desire to praise God or do they go to church because somebody else in the family desires to praise God? Are we practicing our own faith, or someone else's?

What about your personal devotional activities? Does each family member spend regular time reading the Scriptures? Do you pray together? Does each person have his or her own prayer times? How real are these times of meditation? Do you find that often you are just going through the motions by habit, or do you feel a sense of real communion with the Lord?

Would Taras Shevchenko have been satisfied with the spiritual atmosphere of your home?

Our worship—or our lack of it—can tell so much about us. When Jesus calls us to examine our worship habits, he gives us an effective way to check our spiritual oil. When God becomes the center of our lives, our worship comes alive. When our worship goes dead, or even worse, when it becomes mere show, we have a sure clue that God no longer occupies the place he should in our hearts.

Dr. Wiersbe really hooked my attention with one paragraph in his book. As I said earlier, the book is entitled *Real Worship.* Its subtitle promises about real worship: "It will transform your life."

In his preface, Wiersbe wrote:

> I am sure there is one thing we definitely agree on: *You and I personally, and the church collectively, are desperately in need of transformation.* We are weary of "business as usual." We need and want a transforming experience from the Lord, the kind of spiritual visitation that will help to heal our broken homes and our split churches; that will strip away our religious veneer and get us back to reality; that will restore true spiritual values and destroy the cheap counterfeits we have been foisting on ourselves and the lost world; that will, most of all, bring such glory to God that the world will sit up and take notice and confess that "God is truly among you" (1 Corinthians 14:25).

In our personal lives, in our homes, and in the church, Jesus calls us to the transforming power of real worship.

**CHAPTER FIVE**

# HOW GOOD ARE YOU AT FORGIVING?

*For if you forgive men their trespasses, your heavenly Father also will forgive you; but if you do not forgive men their trespasses, neither will your Father forgive your trespasses* (Matthew 6:14-15).

Tears streamed down the face of the woman as she told us her story. All of us in the counseling seminar that day were veteran ministers who had heard every sordid tale known to humanity. But the intensity of this lady's anger made most of us flinch.

"I'll never forgive the _______________!" she wept through clinched teeth. "He told me it was his duty as my father to teach me how to love a man properly. The real result was that I have never been able to love any man since then. I couldn't stand for even my own husband to touch me."

Seldom had we seen hatred so fierce. "Night after night he came to my bed," she explained. "From the time I was 12 or 13 until I finally moved out to get away from him, he forced himself on me. I remember feeling so dirty."

We assured her that in cases like this the fault never lies with the child, but she was deaf to our reassurances. Just as she had been to the words of a dozen counselors during the 20 years since her father had last abused her.

"Why did your mother put up with it?" we inquired.

"She chose to look the other way. He waited until she went to work every night before he came into my bedroom. I suppose he knew she would have to object if he touched me while she was in the house. When I complained to her, and later when I cried about it to some of my teachers, all of them implied that I was making up lies about a good man. They made me feel even worse than I already did. So I soon learned to keep it to myself. I moved out as soon as I could find a place to go."

"Have you had to be around your father since that time?" one of my colleagues asked her.

"When my kids came along, Mom used to call and beg me to bring them home for Thanksgiving or Christmas. I told her I'd come if he was not there. She always whined that she couldn't ask him to leave his own house on a holiday. And she would scold me and tell me to grow up and get over whatever I imagined that he did to me. So the kids and I just stayed away."

Once more the hot, angry tears spilled down her cheeks as she described the alienation that cut her off from her family. "I'll go to my grave hating that evil man," she vowed.

Every waking minute of this woman's adult life she had spent hating her father. Apparently with good cause. Nothing we said to her that day seemed to make even the slightest dent in her resolve to keep on hating the man who had wronged her so horribly.

After years in business with his father and his brothers, something arose between them—something too hot and hard for them to settle amicably, so they forced my friend out of the family business. Right at a time when his kids were reaching those expensive college years, and right at the time when his earning power should have been peaking, my friend found himself unemployed. Out on the street vocationally.

All he had ever done was to run a hardware business. He was good at it. So, when the shock of the family rupture wore off enough for him to think clearly, he set about to open a new hardware store. His own store this time. One he could run as he saw fit.

Like most new store owners, my friend's hours during those start-up days were atrocious. If I happened to be out for some reason way before dawn, I would bump into him at our favorite breakfast place. Several times when my wife and I stopped at a nearby coffee shop late in the evening, we would see this fellow dash in to snatch a to-go order as he headed back to the office to catch up on his ordering or his bookkeeping.

"Did you hear that Jeb Cox died last night?" a friend asked me one morning in the days right before Christmas that year. "They found him dead down at the store. He was working late as usual. Heart attack, they think."

I went to the funeral. You could cut the anger and hurt with a knife. As the dead man's father and brothers and their families filed in, his own sons and daughters glared at them. Those relatives had murdered their father. If they had treated him fairly, he would not have been slaving so hard all those late nights. They killed him.

I saw the icy anger written on their faces and wondered how long it would take for this fractured family to forgive one another. Would there ever be a time when their resentment would soften and allow them to love one another again?

## THE HARDEST COMMAND?

How good are you at forgiving?

Forgiveness is seldom easy.

The hurts done to us by others can sometimes be incredibly severe.

The wounds inflicted on children by their parents and on parents by their offspring often seem to be the hardest of all to forgive.

How good are *you* at forgiving?

In your memory have you buried hard feelings about abuses suffered long ago, hard feelings that come alive fresh and raw in all their ugliness when you encounter the person who wronged you?

Do you stack up little grievances day by day until your hostility toward a close associate or a mate freezes your face or ices over your soul?

How many grudges do you bear?

How much resentment have you stored up?

Have you been mistreated in a way you cannot forget?

The Scriptures are quite clear in their instructions about forgiveness. For those who would serve the Lord and live in his grace, forgiveness is not optional.

"Forgive one another, whenever any of you has a complaint against someone else," the apostle Paul instructs us (Colossians 3:13, GNB). It would be hard to be plainer than that.

Do you recall Jesus' famous requirement that those who offend us are to receive our forgiveness as many as seventy times seven?

Here in the Sermon on the Mount the Master warns us that we may forfeit God's forgiveness for our own sins if we refuse to forgive those who wrong us. This is serious business.

Many Christians say that this may be the hardest commandment God gives us. But the Lord does not lay down this requirement to make life hard for us. Like all of his commands, this one is given for our good. He knows that few things can disrupt our family life or hurt us individually more than refusing to forgive.

**HECTOR'S HABIT**

Every school-day morning I go to a nearby public high school to teach the academic Bible class. Several years ago I was sharing the classroom of a sharp English teacher. On her desk one day I spotted copies of a poem she was teaching to her students, C.A. Trypanis' trenchant piece called "Habit."

As I left the classroom that morning, I snitched a copy of the poem. And I'm glad I did. It is an extraordinarily fine statement of the truth Christ imparts to us about forgiving others.

To help you appreciate the poet's fine lines, let me briefly remind you of the gist of one of Homer's tales in his *Iliad.*

You may recall—if you listened better in high school English class than I did—that the Greek warrior Hector killed Achilles' best buddy Patroclus in a battle. When word reached Achilles that his friend had been slain, he vowed on the spot that he would avenge his friend's death. "Hector will pay," he swore. "I'll get that dirty so-and-so if it's the last thing I ever do."

Finally the day came when Achilles got his wish. He cornered the hated Hector in a battle and made good his threat. Before the battle was done, Hector lay dead in the dust at his feet.

But that was not enough, Achilles found out. His heart was still full of rage at Hector. So he stood there over the body of his enemy and vowed that Hector would never receive a decent burial.

Vengefully, the angry Achilles bored holes just above Hector's heels, behind the tendons. Into those holes he inserted long leather thongs. With them Achilles tied Hector's body to the back of his chariot and dragged him home, face down, with his nose "furrowing the dust" (that's Homer's great line).

In the days that followed, the hate in Achilles' heart continued to rage. It died slowly. "Dawn after dawn," Homer tells us, "Achilles used to harness the fast horses to his chariot, tie Hector loosely to the back of it, and when he had dragged him three times 'round Patroclus' barrow, go back to his hut, leaving the body stretched face downward in the dust" (*Iliad*, xxiv, 46ff).

Few authors have ever excelled Homer's portrait here of an unforgiving heart full of hate. Touched by it, Trypanis the poet has done a masterful job of bringing home its truth for all of us. Do these lines grab your soul, as they do mine?

*It can become a habit every morning*
*To drag broad Hector's body round the tomb,*
*Fling it face downward, and with hollow scorning*
*Return to your beakéd hut, the hours of gloom.*

*It can become a habit, but the heart*
*Will soon forget her barren anger-lust.*
*Only your hands will act the villain part,*
*Only your feet still prod him in the dust.*

*And every day the wrinkle of his smile*
*Will deepen as your rancor leaves no trace,*
*And all the scars, the dirt you wished to pile*
*On Hector, will disfigure your own face.*

The poet is right. Some of us are still dragging around Hector. For us Hector may be a former marriage partner. Or some friend who did us dirt. He may be a long-dead parent. Or a church leader who didn't see things our way.

In our world we can find lots of Hectors. We are forever dragging them around, unwilling to forgive. Thus clinging to our implacable bitterness, the person we hurt worst is us.

## HOW TO DO IT

The bedrock rule for happiness in any home is that we must learn to forgive.

Forgiving is seldom easy, but Jesus gives us some simple, practical suggestions to help us get it done.

*1) Confront the person who has wronged you.*

By "confront" I do not mean "attack." Jesus teaches us that we need to get face-to-face, eyeball-to-eyeball with any person who has offended us. And we need to do it just as soon as possible after the offense.

Jesus counsels us, "If your brother sins against you, go and tell him his fault, between you and him alone. If he listens to you, you have gained a brother" (Matthew 18:15).

The person we are unhappy with deserves this. He or she may not even know we are miffed at them.

While marriage counseling, I have been amazed at how many times one of the mates will register strong I've-been-stepped-on feelings, and their partner will be totally unaware that this particular situation was even a problem.

So Jesus counsels us to talk to the person we need to forgive.

If I am feeling bad toward you, and I go tell somebody else about it first, I have sinned against you. You have a right to hear my complaint against you before anyone else does. Often a simple talk will settle the whole affair.

This may be the reason Jesus instructs us, "If your brother sins against you, rebuke him" (Luke 17:3).

*2) When you feel bad toward another person, do good for him.*

To obey Jesus' instructions, we need to look for specific kindnesses we can do for the person who has mistreated us. Paul was echoing Jesus when he wrote, "If your enemy is hungry, feed him; if he is thirsty, give him a drink" (Romans 12:20). For Jesus teaches us in his great sermon, "I say unto you, Love your enemies, bless them that curse you, do good to them that hate you, and pray for those who despitefully use you" (Matthew 5:44, NKJV).

Christ challenges us here to do the exact opposite of what we feel like doing. He is calling for the redeemed soul to rise above the carnal self.

When we show special kindness and love to a person who has been showing only malice and spitefulness toward us, we accomplish two things: 1) We confuse him. 2) We clear up our own thoughts and emotions.

*3) Be selfish.*

Is there such a thing as enlightened selfishness? I think so.

When you forgive another person, you bless yourself.

This how Jesus says it will be. "Blessed are the merciful, for they shall obtain mercy" (Matthew 5:7). "The measure you give is the measure you get" (Matthew 7:1).

Nothing can clot up our souls and clog up our personal relationships much worse than unresolved resentment.

Nothing can cloud over our happiness much worse than a bellyful of angry, hurt feelings.

Forgiveness is smart. As the Proverbs tell us, "The merciful man doeth good to his own soul" (11:7, KJV).

So be selfish.

Forgive.

*4) Use worship as a reminder to set right all offenses.*

What a clever tactic Jesus recommends here! Those of us in families that are accustomed to worshiping often will never nurse our stubbed feelings for long if we let every worship experience remind us to clear the spiritual deck.

Jesus addressed this idea from two directions.

To the offender, Jesus says in the Sermon on the Mount, "If you are offering your gift at the altar, and there remember that your brother has something against you, leave your gift there before the altar and go; first be reconciled to your brother and then come and offer your gift" (Matthew 5:23-24).

To the offended, Jesus says in Mark 11:25, "When you stand praying (in other words, when you are worshiping), forgive, if you have anything against anyone."

Our Lord's directions here are wise and effective. We should never come to worship without unburdening our souls of every offended feeling. Resentment and hostility should be laid down and left behind whenever we enter God's house. Following this simple rule would prevent us from harboring any long-standing hostility toward a sibling or a parent or a spouse.

*5) Be sure you are forgiven.*

We are now back where we started. Remember Jesus' words that kicked off this chapter? "If you do not forgive men their trespasses, neither will your Father forgive your trespasses" (Matthew 6:15).

This is one way to look at the Scriptures' requirement that we resolve our conflicts with other family members and friends. *We have to forgive in order to be forgiven.* We could lose our souls by refusing to forgive someone who has hurt us.

But a second focus on the subject is also compelling. *We are not likely to be very forgiving unless we feel forgiven.* If you are finding it almost impossible to forgive someone who has hurt you badly—if you just cannot turn loose of those deep feelings of resentment, you may need to look carefully at your own relationship with God. How forgiven do you feel?

Do you remember Jesus' hard-hitting parable about the servant for whom his master forgave a huge debt? It's short and to the point.

*Therefore the kingdom of heaven may be compared to a king who wished to settle accounts with his servants. When he began the reckoning, one was brought to him who owed him ten thousand talents; and as he could not pay, his lord ordered him to be sold, with his wife and children and all that he had, and payment to be made. So the servant fell on his knees, imploring him, "Lord, have patience with me, and I will pay you everything." And out of pity for him the lord of that servant released him and forgave him the debt. But that same servant, as he went out, came upon one of his fellow servants who owed him a hundred denarii; and seizing him by the throat he said, "Pay what you owe." So his fellow servant fell down and besought him, "Have patience with me, and I will pay you." He refused and went and put him in prison till he should pay the debt. When his fellow servants saw what had taken place, they were greatly distressed, and they went and reported to their lord all that had taken place. Then his lord summoned him and said to him, "You wicked servant! I forgave you all that debt because you besought me; and should not you have had mercy on your fellow servant, as I had mercy on you?" And in anger his lord delivered him to the jailers, till he should pay all his debt. So also my heavenly Father will do to every one of you, if you do not forgive your brother from your heart* (Matthew 18:23-35).

Why was the servant so unwilling to forgive? Obviously he did not understand what his master had done for him.

Maybe some of us don't either. Could it be that we refuse to forgive because we feel unforgiven?

If we're going to master this business of forgiving, we need to be absolutely sure that we are right with God ourselves. We set our family relationships right by first getting our own relationship with God right.

*6) If we want to be forgiving, we should imitate Jesus.*

They spat on him
and beat him.
They stripped him
and nailed him to a piece of wood,
and Jesus prayed, "Father, forgive them."

When they did their worst to him, he tried to put it in the best light. He recognized their limited understanding—"They know not what they do"—he said, and forgave them.

Approximately a year later the same Jewish court sentenced righteous Stephen to death. As his accusers threw the fatal stones at him, this good man consciously imitated Jesus. Kneeling down, he prayed for his murderers to be forgiven.

We need to imitate Jesus, too. When people mistreat us and hurt us, we also need to consciously imitate our Savior—and forgive.

This is what the Scriptures call for. "Forgive one another, whenever any of you has a complaint against someone else. You must forgive each other in the same way that the Lord has forgiven you" (Colossians 3:13, GNB).

On more than one occasion my heart has ached when some person I love has dared to share the deepest wounds of their soul, and then has told me with agony etched on their face, "I can never forgive the person who did that to me."

My instant reaction is not to blame them, not to scold them, but to weep inside for them. For I know the frightful price they are paying for the cold anger that freezes their hearts. It has to cast a chill on all their present relationships with innocent family members and friends, people who have no connection to the unforgettable, and seemingly unforgivable, offense.

Yes, it is hard to forgive. But at its core, my refusal to turn loose of past injuries and grudges is selfish. It is a way of saying how badly *I* have been hurt. After what *I* have been through, *I* have a right to *my* anger. This whole nasty thing is basically about me.

If I can ever get *me* out of the picture long enough to see how much damage my perpetual indignation is doing to my relationships with the members of my present family, then hanging on to my bitterness and rehearsing my past pain might no longer appear to be the holy business I have imagined them to be.

Only when I have turned loose of the hurts I have been nursing can I dare to pray as Jesus taught us, "Forgive us our sins, as we forgive those who sin against us."

CHAPTER SIX

# MOTH AND RUST

*Do not lay up for yourselves treasures on earth, where moth and rust consume and where thieves break in and steal, but lay up for yourselves treasures in heaven, where neither moth nor rust consumes and where thieves do not break in and steal. For where your treasure is, there will your heart be also.*

*The eye is the lamp of the body. So, if your eye is sound, your whole body will be full of light; but if your eye is not sound, your whole body will be full of darkness. If then the light in you is darkness, how great is the darkness!*

*No one can serve two masters; for either he will hate the one and love the other, or he will be devoted to the one and despise the other. You cannot serve God and mammon.*

*Therefore I tell you, do not be anxious about your life, what you shall eat or what you shall drink, nor about your body, what you shall put on. Is not life more than food, and the body more than clothing? Look at the birds of the air: they neither sow nor reap nor gather into barns, and yet your heavenly Father feeds them. Are you not of more value than they? And which of you by being anxious can add one cubit to his span of life? And why are you anxious about clothing? Consider the lilies of the field, how they grow; they neither toil nor spin; yet I tell you, even Solomon in all his glory was not arrayed like one of these. But if God so clothes the grass of the field, which today is alive and tomorrow is thrown into the oven, will he not much more clothe you, O men of little faith? Therefore do not be anxious, saying, "What shall we eat?" or "What shall we drink?" or "What shall we wear?" For the Gentiles seek all these things; and your heavenly Father knows that you need them all. But seek first his kingdom and his righteousness, and all these things shall be yours as well.*

*Therefore do not be anxious about tomorrow, for tomorrow will be anxious for itself. Let the day's own trouble be sufficient for the day* (Matthew 6:19-34).

## HOMES THAT LAST

I love a story I found years ago in an issue of *Our Daily Bread.*

The alumni association of a large university sent out survey forms to their former students. They wanted to see how successful these students had turned out to be.

Somewhat soggy and several weeks late, one of the survey forms finally found its way to a man who was now serving as a missionary in the tribal lands of Columbia in South America.

Here is how he answered their questions:

1) Do you own your own home? *Yes.* (Years before he paid the tribal people $125 for a palm-thatched shelter in the Amazon basin.)

2) Do you rent quarters elsewhere? *Yes.* (Once or twice a year, when he and his family attend missionary conferences for the workers in that part of the world, they pay their part of the cost to stay in a house where all the mission families are crammed in together.)

3) Do you own a boat? *Yes.* (The missionary's dugout canoe can usually be found along the riverbank just south of his hut.)

4) Do you plan to travel abroad during the next two years? *Yes.* (They will probably be going home on a brief furlough if mission funds permit it during the coming year.)

5) What is your income? *Under $10,000 a year.*

6) How many automobiles do you own? *None.*

How do you suppose the university computer handled those answers? The survey-takers obviously had not taken into account either the lifestyle or the kind of wealth this mission family had found in serving their Lord. Probably the computer spat out the missionary's answers with a notation that said, "Data incompatible."

## FAMILY TREASURE

What the world adds up as wealth is so often incompatible with our Lord's evaluation. "Do not lay up for yourselves treasures on earth, where moth and rust consume and where thieves break in and steal," Jesus says to a world full of people desperately trying to "get ahead." Instead, he says, "Lay up for yourselves treasures in heaven."

Where is your family's treasure? I cannot ask you a more important question, for Jesus is correct when he warns that "where your treasure is, there will your heart be also."

When I ask where your family has laid up its treasures, I am not asking if your family is rich or poor by worldly standards. That really has little to do with the answer. I know some very rich people who have devoted their lives to laying up heavenly treasures, and I know some food stamp recipients who have no higher aim in life than buying a bigger TV or a newer car.

How much money we have is not the subject of our Lord's sermon. When he talks about where we lay up our treasures, he is calling us to take inventory about what matters most to us in life.

So I ask you again: Where are the treasures of your family?

- As you have raised your children, have you placed more importance on their financial and professional future than on their future faithfulness to the church and to the Lord?
- When your family unexpectedly has extra cash in hand, do you spend it all on your own comfort and pleasure, or do you set aside a good part of it for the Lord's work?
- As you make retirement plans, how does your concern for the future of the church stack up against your concern for your own financial future?
- How does your family's annual budget for travel and play compare to your annual allotment for the hungry and the homeless? (You do remember how James defined "pure religion," don't you?)
- Would you get more pleasure out of buying another CD than you would from providing the financial needs of a fruitful mission program?
- Do you give as much money each year to the church as you spend on cigarettes? Or on panty hose? Or on video rentals? Or on coffee and cokes?
- How often have you let a chance at some overtime or the chance of a promotion steal the hours you might have spent training your children or helping some elderly friend?
- When you think about taking on heavy new payments for something you probably could live without, how much do you consider the impact of this new financial drain on your ability to do what the Lord wants you to be doing as a family in his Kingdom?

## EMPTY HANDS

I could go on asking meddlesome questions like these for a long time, but it wouldn't be much fun for me or for you either. Does taking this sort of an inventory help us to be more accountable to our Lord's restriction against laying up treasures on earth? Or do questions like these succeed only in ruffling our submerged guilt and making us a bit angry with the meddler who dares to ask them?

It is hard to warn a materialistic people about their materialism without sounding self-righteous or condemning. In fact, this love affair our generation has going with bigger and better and newer possessions may be the hardest subject for a preacher to broach today.

Years ago when Nita and I finally got all our kids through school, our budget eased up enough for us to make some purchases we had been putting off for a long time. Within the same year our family bought new carpet (the first in eighteen years), a new car (the first in twenty years), and a new TV. I joked to some of my minister colleagues that with all these new purchases, I was fast running out of things to preach against!

But it really is not a joking matter. Our Lord was dead serious when he warned that his people cannot serve two masters. We will "hate the one and love the other," he said. We "cannot serve God and mammon."

If we have any doubt what Jesus meant by this, we would do well to read his warnings in a newer Bible version. The New International Version, for example, leaves no question when it plainly translates, "You cannot serve both God and Money"—with a capital *M*.

But lots of us have tried to serve both—to our sorrow. Lots of us *are* trying it right now—and we are certain to bump our spiritual heads. You cannot do it, Jesus said. The blessings of heaven have a way of slipping out of our grasp when we open our hands to grab all the blessings of this world.

Politicians agonize today about the plight of the poor. Christians have always shared this concern. But I tell you with an aching heart that far more Christians have been lost by Jesus because they had too much money than because they had too little. Far more Christian families have fallen apart under the burden of wealth than under the pressures of poverty.

We know this, but knowing it does not keep many of us from continuing to chase the almighty dollar as if it were the solution to all that ails us.

I raise questions about our love of money, not to condemn those who hear me, but to sound the warning—however futilely—to a generation racing hell-bent toward a precipice of ruin and disillusionment. If my message rings with the urgency of rebuke and reproach, this is true only because I recognize myself as one caught up in the same fatal, foolish race.

Stridently the apostle Paul raised the same cry of caution. "Those who desire to be rich fall into temptation, into a snare, into many senseless and hurtful desires that plunge men into ruin and destruction. For the love of money is the root of all evils," he explained. "It is through this craving that some have wandered away from the faith and pierced their hearts with many pangs" (1 Timothy 6:9-10).

Is this what we want?

## THE CLEAR VIEW

James Michener wrote truly when he said, "If gold dazzles, it also blinds." When our hearts are fired by visions of wealth, our eyes are glazed and our minds are deluded by false dreams of happiness. Dreaming of having so much, we can easily wind up with nothing worth having.

This gold-induced blindness that dupes us into wasting our lives may be exactly what Jesus has in mind in this section of the Sermon on the Mount. He talks first about where we should lay up our treasures. Later he tells us how impossible it is to serve both God and Money. Tucked in between those sets of verses are his puzzling words about our eyes.

All the light we have inside our bodies comes through our eyes, Jesus points out. That is what eyes are for, to let in light. And if our eyes are fouled up, we're going to have only darkness inside us. The blinding flash of the gold, for instance, will not illuminate our hearts; it will damage our eyesight and leave us full of darkness. And Jesus says, "How great will be that darkness!"

The poet Robert Service said it far better than I can.

**HOMES THAT LAST**

*I wanted the gold and I got it—*
*Came out with a fortune last fall.*
*Yet somehow life's not what I thought it,*
*And somehow the gold isn't all.*

What a tragedy if we learn that too late!

My backbone still shivers when I remember the news report in the Las Vegas *Sun* just a few days before Liberace died. According to Paul Harvey, the newspaper reported that Liberace had "a fortune in jewelry and paintings, seven luxurious homes, twenty cars, eighteen pianos, and AIDS."

Most of us will never possess that kind of wealth, but we suffer from the same deadly sort of blindness if we choose to ignore the will of God while we chase paltry possessions that do not really matter when all is said and done.

**REAL WORTH**

Once a year, if I gave him half a chance, my good Christian banker Noel Bruce used to ask me to update my paperwork in his files. With a twinkle in his eye he shoved the bank's forms at me one day and said, "Preacher, let's find out what you're worth."

Both of us understood what he meant. He wanted that pesky piece of paper filled out so he could keep the bank examiners happy. Both he and I knew, of course, that you can't measure a person's true worth with figures on a balance sheet. Lots of people don't know that. They constantly weigh life on an economic scale. In fact, some people recognize no other measure.

The historian Will Durant was sometimes prone to see his own world when he looked at ages long past. I suspect that he lapsed into that fallacy when he described the thinking of the Romans a century and a half before Jesus. "Everyone longed for money," he wrote. "Everyone judged or was judged in terms of money."

Was Durant describing our age as well? I hope not. All of us need some money to survive in our society, but having a lot of it or having a little offers no dependable barometer of whether a person is good or smart or respectable or happy. Wasn't it Jesus who said, "A man's life does not consist in the abundance of his possessions"?

Have you noticed that when we meet a long-lost friend and he asks us, "How are you getting along?" we are prone to answer him first in terms of health or money? "Oh, I guess I'm all right. I own two Cadillacs, and we just moved into a bigger house, and my business showed a solid profit last year. . . ."

"I don't mean that," the friend may reply. "How are you really getting along?"

Then, with furrowed brow, we get down to the real truth about the quality of our lives. We talk about relationships in our families, about the people who stress us and bless us, about the people who look up to us and love us. We talk about our fears and our hopes and our hurts and our faith. And on that level of living, we find out that money really doesn't have much to do with "how we're getting along."

Then, perhaps, we understand the words of the apostle Paul when he said, "godliness, with contentment, is great gain."

If we have bombed out on the most precious relationships in our lives, no amount of money can replace what we have lost.

A man who made a ton of money the year before I met him sobbed as he told me his story. With tears streaming down his face he recalled how his 20-year-old daughter cursed him as she screamed her rejection of both him and his faith.

The same week another well-to-do man told me the anguished tale of seeing his brilliant older son sentenced to the penitentiary for embezzling municipal funds.

Both of these wealthy fathers would have given up their fortunes gladly to have their children back on solid ground and to know the contentment Paul talked about. They were far from content. They lived in torment, wondering what it was in their own values that disposed their offspring to go so sadly astray.

When I sit down each year to compute my net worth for my banker, I write down on the plus side my house, my cars, my insurance, my investments, along with what little money I might have in his bank. Then

I realize how little all of these material things are worth compared to the things in my life that really matter.

Most of us waste endless anxieties over the things that hardly matter. How much we need to hear the words of Jesus: "Your heavenly Father knows that you need those things. Seek first his kingdom and his righteousness, and all these things shall be yours as well."

## THE BEST BEQUEST

If we listened well in the fourth grade, we usually remember Patrick Henry as a great patriot who stood bravely when our nation fought for her freedom. But Patrick Henry was more than that. He was also a Christian father.

In his will, he made all the usual provisions for the members of his family—to one of them this piece of property, to another, this sum of money, and so forth. At the end of his will he wrote these words:

*I have now disposed of all my property to my family. There is one thing more that I wish I could give them: that is the Christian religion. If they had that, and I had not given them one shilling, they would have been rich; and if they had not that, and I had given them the world, they would be poor.*

What are you leaving to your family?

**CHAPTER SEVEN**

# DON'T CRITICIZE!

*Judge not, that you be not judged. For with the judgment you pronounce you will be judged, and the measure you give will be the measure you get. Why do you see the speck that is in your brother's eye, but do not notice the log that is in your own eye? Or how can you say to your brother, "Let me take the speck out of your eye," when there is the log in your own eye? You hypocrite, first take the log out of your own eye, and then you will see clearly to take the speck out of your brother's eye* (Matthew 7:1-5).

Of all the instruction Jesus gave in the Sermon on the Mount, could any part of it have more impact on the quality of life in our homes than his opening words in Matthew 7?

"Judge not, that you be not judged," we read in our more familiar versions of the Bible.

Phillips' paraphrase brings the teaching home where we live. Here Jesus says, "Don't criticise people, and you will not be criticised. For you will be judged by the way you criticise others, and the measure you give will be the measure you receive."

Some of us by nature are more critical than others, and we make it tough on others. It is no fun to live with a critic.

I like the story about the woman who hired a medium to bring back the spirit of her dead husband. The seance worked. When his ghost came floating into the darkened room, she got so excited. "Honey," she asked, "is it really better up there?" "Oh, yes," he replied, "it is much better. But I'm not up there!"

Chances are good that this poor fellow spent his days married to a critic.

How often do you criticize?

If you are a man, do you find something wrong with every meal your wife cooks?

Do you often point out the flaws in your wife's methods of housekeeping or kid-raising or love-making?

Man or woman, do you often find fault with the way your mate handles your family's money? Does this topic generate lots of criticism in your home?

What about your feelings toward the people who live next door and across the street? Are most of your comments about them negative and critical?

What about the people who serve you—your paper carrier, your mail carrier, your grocery store checkout lady, your service station attendant, and your dry cleaning clerk? Are they all dummies? Is that the general gist of your remarks about them?

Just how critical are you? Is criticism your normal reaction to the people and circumstances around you?

When you go to a restaurant, is the food usually good? Or do you almost always find some fault with it? Is the service usually acceptable, or do you make life miserable for most of the waiters and waitresses who serve you? Are they glad when they see you coming back?

What is your basic feeling about school teachers and principals and coaches and choir directors and other folks who must deal with your children? Have they been a favorite target of your wrath?

What about the people you have to work with and for? Are they competent people who merit your respect, or do you look at most of them as stumble-bums who seldom do anything right? Do they enjoy working with you?

Do your children enjoy your approval? Do they feel like they please you most of the time? Or do your kids live with the unremitting burden of your criticism? Would you enjoy having you for a parent?

Just how much does your criticism affect your family? Your neighbors? Your church? Your office? Are folks glad when you show up, or do they run from you like people avoiding a black cloud?

I ask these questions not to brand you as a critic, but to help you face the truth if you are one. The role of "Critic" is an unhappy part to play, and on the stage of life it creates a ton of misery for the captive members of your cast.

Jesus spoke no wiser words than this simple command, "Don't criticize!"

**GOOD INTENTIONS**

Let us give the critic his or her due. At least in Christian circles, most criticizers mean well. This fact does not make their continual criticisms any holier or healthier or any easier to endure, but it does let us recognize that our critics are usually not bad people. They simply use rotten methods to improve their world.

The inveterate critics in churches, for example, usually have the church's best interests at heart. This has been my experience, anyway. These critical people love the church and want it to grow. They want the church to be fruitful and to excel in all areas of its ministry. Unfortunately, though, the critics' method of achieving these ends will likely produce the opposite result. They hurt the church they love.

From our perspective centuries later, we can see how grievously Paul's critics wounded the church of their day. At a time when Christianity was sweeping the globe, Paul had to turn his attention and energy away from evangelizing to deal with brethren who kept finding fault with what he preached and how he preached and to whom he preached.

On every hand this great man of God encountered some zealot who did not like his methods or his message. Probably Paul's in-house critics were among the best-read and most active members of the early church. Because they sincerely believed that Paul's ministry flew in the face of God's rules as they understood them, they hounded him day after day.

Who can begin to estimate how many more people Paul might have converted and how many more churches he might have planted had it not been for those critics who blindly thought they were helping the Lord's church?

The same thing is true about many critics in the home or in the office. They criticize because what goes on in the home or in the company really matters to them. Desperately they want the people around them to perform well. But their faultfinding often causes people to perform worse.

I know a mother who has alienated her children by her sharp tongue and her sour temper. She wants her family to be active in the church, but her continual criticism of the people at the church has taught her kids to have little respect for anybody there. Today they stay away.

This same lady wants her kids to do well at school, so she has set high standards for their schoolwork from first grade on. The high hurdles on their track have been really high, and in their mother they have had a tough coach. Diligently she has called attention to every wrong motion they have made. Every misstep has drawn her reproof.

She was the only one surprised when her children quickly tired of the competition and found something other than studies to occupy their minds.

This mother loves her kids more than anything else in the whole world, but by her constant criticism she has destroyed their happiness and soured their lives. Because of her criticism the kids she loves so much have felt unloved most of the time. Today she is paying a high price for this. She means well, but the measure she has given is now the measure she gets from her children, just as Jesus predicted.

In the days right after David Brinkley died, Cal Thomas reminisced in his newspaper column about his lengthy friendship with the famous newsman. He told about the time when he interviewed Brinkley on a TV show shortly after the newscaster had published his memoirs. They discussed Brinkley's renowned career and Thomas told him what an honor it was for his former flunky to host his hero and mentor as a guest on the show.

"I mentioned that his late mother kept popping up in the book and that she seemed to withhold her approval from him. I asked him if he and his mother had reconciled before her death.

"He said, 'No, but not because I didn't try.'

"'David, she should have been proud of you,' I said.

"'I thought so, too,' he replied, as tears filled his eyes. It was a rare look into the heart of David Brinkley."

No criticism wounds as severely as that offered by a parent.

A year or so ago I decided to fill in one of the major missing segments of my education. For the first time in my life, I read Tolstoy's *War and Peace.* Princess Maria's irascible father was an inveterate critic who made life miserable for his daughter. Nothing she did could please him.

Tolstoy says the man "took special pains not only to insult and humiliate her, but to make her feel that she was always and forever in the wrong."

Is this how your children perceive your parental efforts to correct their mistakes?

All of us know the old saying about the road that is paved with good intentions. Remember where it leads? Critics with good intentions will almost always get us there.

In his fine commentary on Acts, Dr. Lloyd Ogilvie tells of a time in his ministry when critics were dragging him down. He would dwell for days on one cranky comment about a sermon, totally forgetting all the complimentary remarks of his members. "One rejection," Dr. Ogilvie wrote, "can tip the scales weighted with hundreds of affirmations. Satan's trick is to preoccupy us with a rejection so that we forget the positive responses."

Few people are more available to accomplish Satan's purposes than critics—no matter how good their intentions.

## THE POWER OF PRAISE

Sincere praise is the opposite of criticism. Technically, I suppose, we might obey Jesus' command, "Judge not," if we just kept our mouths shut and met others with silence—although silence can sometimes be the harshest judgment of all. Have we obeyed the spirit of Christ's instructions about criticism, though, if we simply refrain from making derogatory remarks about others? I doubt it.

I grant you that the slant of our Lord's teaching on this subject is very much like the slant of this chapter so far: it deals negatively with the person who is prone to judge his brother. It tells him *not* to do it. Jesus even goes so far as to say, "You hypocrite!" as he admonishes the self-appointed judge to clean up his own act before he inspects somebody else's.

Few people would quarrel with our Lord's assertion that critical people usually have more than enough problems to deal with in their own lives. Jesus says they need to extract the tree limbs from their own eyes before they set out to remove sawdust specks from the eyes of others. It's a good illustration, but it still reflects only the negative side of the subject of judging.

What about the positive side? If we resolve to stop being critical of other people, is that the end of the matter? Or should we not go on to replace the misguided spirit of judging with the enlightened spirit of encouraging and praising others?

Mark Twain once said, "I can live for two months on a good compliment." Most of us can.

As much as our bodies need protein and calories to survive, our spirits need affirmation and approval. Without evidence that somebody somewhere approves of who we are and of what we are doing, our souls soon wither.

Do you remember when the hottest book on the market was Dr. Thomas Harris' work entitled *I'm OK—You're OK*? One way I have of knowing that I'm O.K. is for you to tell me so. It helps a great deal if I hear that same message from my mother and my father and my brothers and my sisters and my aunts and my uncles and my cousins and my teachers and my neighbors and my buddies and my mail carrier.

Most of all, of course, I need to hear it from God. That is why it is so vital for all of us who are in Christ to understand and to experience God's grace. We need to know that we are approved by him all the time. Then we're really O.K.

Do you see what an important part you and I play in assuring each other of our O.K.-ness? If I am all the time critical of you, I convey the opposite message. But I can do wonders to encourage and bless your life if I take the time to notice the things you do right and to praise you for them.

For raw eloquence and sheer impact few phrases surpass the four words of an old cowboy. All night long he had struggled alongside a Hereford cow as she gave birth to twins. With the first rays of morning light stealing into the old barn, the cowboy patted the hindquarters of the cow as she licked her pair of newborns, and he drawled to that weary mama, "Honey, you done good!" That's a pretty good line to use on the people we care about.

The power of praise may surpass any other force we can employ for the good of our world.

## THE REAL THING

If you are familiar with Paul's letters to the Colossians and to Philemon, you know that the apostle began both letters with a series of compliments to his readers. "We always thank God for you," he would tell them.

Can you say anything nicer about somebody? Can a mother or father say anything finer to a child than this? "I always thank God for you."

What was Paul specifically thankful for in the lives of his readers? He had heard about their strong faith and about their love for others in the Lord's Body, so he hastened to commend them for these fine qualities.

When we hear good reports about members of our families, are we quick to repeat those commendations? If we hear bad reports, we never fail to repeat them. Why not the good ones, too?

"Johnny, your teacher tells me that you talk too much." You can bet your bottom dollar that Johnny will hear about that! "Johnny, your teacher tells me that your reading has really improved." What a tragedy if Johnny should fail to hear that!

The good things we hear about our loved ones can be our finest source of compliments. Paul's letters teach us that.

But they also teach us something even more important about the praise we offer to our loved ones: Paul's compliments were always genuine. "We never used words of flattery," he reminded his converts in Thessalonica.

Flattery is dishonest praise. It is praise gone sour. It always leaves a bad taste and does more harm than good.

When we flatter someone, we leave them feeling used. When we compliment them for something they have done that is genuinely praiseworthy, we leave them feeling good about us and about themselves. Real compliments accomplish real good.

## THE OTHER SIDE

The flipside of our Lord's command not to judge can be heard in Paul's exhortation in 1 Thessalonians 5:11, where he wrote, "Therefore encourage one another and build up one another."

Most families in middle-class America have more than enough critics on board. (Has it ever occurred to you that the critical spirit may be a bigger problem for us in our upwardly mobile, success-oriented culture than it is in a society where people have much less and never expect to have more?) In some of our homes every person present is a critic. Their main pastime is finding fault with one another. It's a deadly atmosphere to live in—one guaranteed to foster divorce and delinquency and devilishness of all sorts.

"Encourage one another and build up one another," the Bible says. By its very nature, criticism is destructive, but praise builds us up. I challenge you to use the art of praise to build up your family.

*Your Mate.* Use carefully chosen compliments to strengthen your marriage. Notice the things your mate does right—the things you like. And mention them.

Don't expect your mate to be a mind reader. If you like something your wife or husband does, say so. The right sort of words can "impart grace to those who hear," the Bible tells us. Impart grace to your mate.

*Your Children.* With words of genuine praise, encourage your children and assure them of your esteem for each one of them. Are you grateful that your teenage son doesn't do drugs? Tell him. Are you pleased that your four-year-old can now handle her potty needs alone? Tell her. Does it delight you when your little ones show an interest in the Lord and in the Scriptures? Be sure they know how you feel.

*Your Parents.* Kids, have you ever thought about making your home a better place by praising your parents? It will work. If you want more chocolate pie, praise the cook when she bakes it! If you want more personal freedom, thank your father for showing trust in you whenever he does. That works so much better than throwing a fit when he doesn't. I'm not talking about being manipulative. I'm talking about speaking honest, genuine words of appreciation whenever your parents' actions or attitudes please you. Words like that will bless both your parents and you. And the Bible is right—they will "build up" your family.

## AN ENCOURAGER

Years ago at our church we had an elder named Bob Muir. He has gone to be with the Lord now, and I miss him—for lots of reasons. Most of all I miss Bob because he was an encourager.

Long ago I lost count of the notes Bob mailed to me. They weren't fancy. They were seldom more than a few lines. But those lines, often scribbled on whatever paper Bob found handy, were filled with words of encouragement.

"Thanks for what you said Sunday about. . . ."

"I thought you did a good job when you. . . ."

With those simple words of gratitude and praise, Bob built me up, just as Paul commanded.

And I was not the only one receiving his notes. Lots of our people heard from Bob. During his years among us, he was our Barnabas—our "son of encouragement," as the Bible called that great man.

Every church needs one. Every family needs one. Could it be that this is God's job for you?

## CHAPTER EIGHT

# PEARLS AND PIGS

*Do not give dogs what is sacred; do not throw your pearls to pigs. If you do, they may trample them under their feet, and then turn and tear you to pieces* (Matthew 7:6, NIV).

We live in an equal-opportunity age, where most jobs no longer are gender-specific and the legal playing field for men and women in the marketplace has been leveled. But when I am trying to apply the Sermon on the Mount to family matters, and in that context I hear Jesus warning us about tossing our pearls to pigs, one form of domestic distress immediately flashes across the screen to my mind, and this particular problem is distinctly feminine.

Over the past four decades I have preached in dozens of churches, often visiting these congregations for seminars or revival times. Through the years the privilege of returning to many of them for repeat engagements has allowed me to establish cherished friendships in churches all across the land.

Repeatedly during my years of ministry, in virtually all of these churches, some dear soul, urgent in her faith in the Lord and her love for his word, has come to me with agony on her face and anguish in her soul. The conversations have been surprisingly the same.

"I'm at my wit's end. I just don't know what I'm going to do. For twenty (or thirty, or forty) years now I have tried everything I know to try and I just cannot get my husband to attend church with me (or to accept Christ)."

Almost every time, the woman hurries to assure me, "I don't mean to leave the wrong impression. My husband is a good man. He's decent and dependable. He's loving and kind. But I just can't seem to get him interested in spiritual things." Then, often with tears about to overflow, she plaintively asks, "What do you think I should do?"

What should I tell her?

My first impulse is to say, "Nothing. Don't say anything. Don't do anything. Give your man some spiritual space. Let him breathe. Get off his case."

Usually I am not quite that blunt, because invariably these are dear, sweet ladies who love the Lord and their husbands with all their hearts. I don't want to bruise them and add to their soul-pain. Somehow, though, I do need to convince them to quit trying so hard to convert their husbands.

Past experience tells me that in situations like these we may never win these men to the Lord unless their wives are wise enough to back off.

To put it most simply, these anxious ladies usually are compounding their problem by violating Jesus' warning not to cast their pearls to pigs. Since it might appear that I was insulting their fine husbands by referring to them as pigs, I would hesitate to use Jesus' metaphor in responding to their concerns. But these well-meaning ladies are complicating their lives by ignoring the principle Jesus sets before us here.

The apostle Peter expressed the same sentiment in softer words. "Likewise you wives," he counseled, "be submissive to your husbands, so that some, though they do not obey the word, *may be won without a word* by the behavior of their wives, when they see your reverent and chaste behavior" (1 Peter 3:1-2).

## SILENT WITNESS

In all of God's word it would be hard to find wiser advice for those of us who have spouses (or parents, or in-laws) who have not yet accepted Jesus. The same Scriptures that tell us to proclaim the gospel and to be ready always to give an answer for the hope that is in us also instruct us to learn the effective strategy of silent witnessing.

We hear this emphasis in the four main metaphors Jesus uses to describe the evangelistic influence of his people: salt, light, leaven, and fire—the first two of them directly from the Sermon on the Mount.

- *"Salt."* "You are the salt of the earth" (Matthew 5:13).
- *"Light."* "You are the light of the world . . . a city set on a hill" (Matthew 5:14-16).
- *"Leaven."* "The kingdom of heaven is like leaven which a woman took and hid in three measures of flour, till it was all leavened" (Matthew 13:33).
- *"Fire."* "I have come to cast fire on the earth" (Luke 12:49).

Note that all four of these are quiet influences. You know the salt is in the gravy, but you can't hear it at work. Light can flood into a dark room without making a sound. "A little yeast works through the whole batch of dough," Paul observed (Galatians 5:9, NIV), but leaven works its fermenting magic without a snap, crackle, or pop. Fire may dance brilliantly on a candle's wick and melt the hardest wax without a whisper.

So it may be that our most effective witnessing for the Lord—savoring, illuminating, leavening, warming the souls of our loved ones—may be accomplished by a winsome quietness, just as Peter said, "Without a word."

Notice, too, that all four of these metaphorical influences work from within. Keep the salt in the shaker and the gravy will be tasteless. Lights outside a room still leave the interior dark. Yeast all by itself on a refrigerator shelf remains inert, lifeless. It works only when it is in the lump of dough. Fire penetrates and probes to the very heart of a log, drawing energy from its core components. Even so, we touch hearts with the message of God's grace most profoundly when we live quiet lives of faith and integrity within the family or social unit. We are far more likely to get across the Lord's message to our loved ones than may some stranger standing outside our circle shouting instructions to the lost.

Jesus expanded these metaphors to sound a warning note about how easily we can mute our witness for him. If salt were to become unsalty, he noted, then it would be no more useful than sand on the footpath. The brightest lamp can be put under a "bushel" (to use the old King James expression). It can be hooded so that its light no longer illuminates the house. Obviously, any fire can burn itself out. "Fire that does not spread must go out," Dr. Elton Trueblood commented. When we stop touching other lives and winning other souls to the Lord, the vitality of our faith has waned. We are saltless salt, darkened lights, dead yeast, dying fires.

The Scriptures recognize that many Christians will live in families which include those who have not accepted Jesus. In 1 Corinthians 7 the apostle Paul tells wives who are married to unbelieving mates to stay in these marriages if their spouses make it possible. "If any woman has a husband who is an unbeliever, and he consents to live with her, she should not divorce him," the apostle wrote. And he spoke positively of the holy influence a Christian may have on the non-Christian members in the faith-blended family. He said, "The unbelieving husband is consecrated through his wife, and the unbelieving wife is consecrated through her husband. Otherwise, your children would be unclean, but as it is they are holy" (7:13-14).

Jesus clearly intends for all who follow him to be drawing others into the circle of faith. It goes without saying, of course, that all of us want most of all to reach the members of our own families. We long for our mates and children to love and obey the Lord we serve. Our hearts burn with the compelling desire for our parents and siblings to walk in the Lord's light. But if we are not careful, the intensity of our yearning for their salvation may make us too aggressive and strident in our efforts to bring them to Christ.

Zeal alone is never enough. In fact, it may hurt more than it helps. To be effective in witnessing to our dearest loved ones we have to use good sense. Nagging is never attractive, even when we do it in the name of the Lord. Answering questions that have not been asked and giving advice that has not been sought seldom is successful—not any more than trying to feed a person who is not hungry. Often our best strategy for evangelizing our loved ones turns out to be patient, faithful silence.

## MOTHERS TO THE RESCUE

During the days when I am writing these words, I am praying alongside three Christian couples I love. They don't know each other, but I know all of them. All three are heartbroken because sons or daughters they raised in the Lord have strayed in their mature years into life-ruining sins and now seem deaf to their parents' concerns for their happiness and for their souls.

In cases like these, the mothering instinct seems to be the same universally. All three of these mothers want to rush in and "fix" things for their grown-up babies. Their immediate response would be to jump on an airplane and fly to the side of their hurting child. They are "rescuers" at heart.

Fathers may have an even stronger desire to attack the problems that threaten their offspring, but in these three cases, at least, the men seem more likely to confront the issues by asserting their authority, while their wives seem more inclined to extend some sort of comfort and care.

I don't know how these tragic real-life stories will play out. One of the three mothers has begun to attend Al-Anon meetings, seeking wisdom and strength to help her handle the desperation she feels for her drug-using son. There she has found other mothers dealing with similar tragedies, and they are helping her to learn the hard art of embracing her son with tough love.

This grieving mother says the support of others going through similar anguish has helped her be wiser and stronger than she ever could have been alone. Without her new Al-Anon friends to encourage and guide her, she long ago would have barged into her grown son's life with ready-made answers and quick fixes. And in his present wrong-headedness, he likely would have trampled her, along with all her well-intentioned pearls of maternal wisdom.

One of the three couples did take off time from their jobs to fly hundreds of miles to their daughter's side. She had been their "perfect" child—the one whose faith had always been so fervent and whose behavior had been exemplary. By accident they learned to their horror that this model daughter had decided to turn her back on Christian morals and "live with" her boyfriend at college.

Later they told me how this once-compliant girl stonewalled their futile efforts to straighten up her life. "We talked for hours," the father confided. "Half of one night we sat with her trying to show her how foolish and out-of-character this lifestyle was for her, but we wasted our words. She didn't hear anything we said."

She didn't need to. She already knew everything her parents thought about her immoral relationship. If all they could do was preach to her, they might as well have stayed home and saved the cost of their plane tickets. At that moment her hormones spoke more loudly than her parents' homilies. Mom and Dad told her the truth, of course, but she wasn't listening.

Is it ever any different when we find ourselves "preaching" to a stubborn family member? In almost every instance the person we target with our words knows our thoughts and beliefs. Most unbelieving husbands know how their Christian wives feel about the church and the Bible and the Lord. They don't need to hear it again. Most older kids are fully aware of their parents' beliefs about sex, drugs, booze, tobacco, tattoos, clothing (or the lack thereof), curfews, tongue-piercing, pornography, loud music, profanity, and predestination. Additional sermons on these topics and dozens of others will not likely increase their awareness of their parents' moral and doctrinal preferences. Especially in tense moments, our verbal exchanges on such matters likely do more harm than good.

### JESUS' PRESCRIPTION

Silent witnessing may be the hardest kind, especially when we know some truth that would save a loved one a lot of heartache and woe. Much of the time, though, our silent lives of courage and faith and kindness and integrity may be the only message our loved ones can hear.

We can go on speaking and risk alienating our blood-kin forever. Or we can win them to Jesus the biblical way—"without a word." Casting our pearls to those who do not value them may get us trampled by the very people we most want to bless.

I'll never forget one lunch invitation I received in a small-town church where I often preached in my younger years. During my months of infrequent preaching for these good people, I had become aware of an older lady who always came to worship alone. While standing at the church door every Sunday, shaking the hands of the departing saints—doing the "preacher thing" when worship was over, I noticed that this lady's husband was always parked along the curb across the street, patiently waiting to ferry her home. I'd waved at him a time or two, and he always smiled and waved back. That was the most contact I'd had with the man until that Sunday when his wife surprised my wife and me by inviting us home with them for lunch.

As we entered their comfortable old home for the first time, lots of subtle signs told me that this house had not seen much company in recent years. By modern standards it was a small house, but these folks were not paupers. Their home was furnished elegantly.

This unusual little lady scurried through the dining room, hastily unloading stacks of magazines and letter-writing stuff and some recently used oil painting supplies from the fine French provincial dining table. Across the shiny mahogany tabletop she whisked a fine lace cloth—much too fine for a klutz like me to eat on, I thought. And soon she covered that dainty cloth with steaming bowls of delicious food that must have been simmering or baking while I was preaching my sermon that morning. It smelled so good!

As I said, these people were not used to having guests. Just finding the proper chairs for each of us at the table required some awkward deliberations on their part. After a couple of false starts, we did manage to get seated—with the Christian lady I didn't really know all that well sitting on the long side of the table nearest the kitchen (she would play hostess all meal long), with my wife across from her, and with her husband and me at opposite ends of the rather long, formal table.

Since the church attender/wife/hostess/cook was also obviously in charge of all matters of a spiritual nature in that home, she instructed me, the visiting preacher, to lead the blessing for the food. Without waiting to see if I was willing, she ducked her head and the rest of us followed suit, bowing during my brief and utterly unremarkable prayer for our food.

Then, before our heads were upright again and before the echoes of my "Amen" had faded, the intense lady of that house knocked off my socks. She fixed me with her hard, black eyes and asked bluntly, "Gene, don't you think my husband is going to hell?"

I was aghast. That she would assault the poor man in this way before virtual strangers told me what agonies she must be putting him through in private. That she would try to enlist my aid in spiritually mugging her man made me horribly uncomfortable.

To this day I have no idea what I replied to her question as I tried to keep from both offending her and abusing him at the same time. He must have sensed that I was desperately trying to shield him from his piranha mate. Instantly he warmed up to me and we enjoyed a most congenial visit during that strange meal.

To my knowledge, that harried little man went to his grave unbaptized.

I was about to say *despite* his wife's feverish efforts to convert him to Christ, but it likely would be more accurate to say that he died outside the faith *because* of her attempts to Christianize him. With a remarkably sweet spirit—in fact, with genial, good humor—he rebuffed her relentless, high-pressure tactics to save his soul. The only way he could survive the intensity of her evangelistic zeal was to keep her at all times at a safe distance. If he weakened his resistance even a smidgen, he knew instinctively that her zeal would consume him.

After years of playing these sharply defined roles, neither of these good people would have known what to do if he had shown even a flicker of interest in Christ or the church. Without knowing it, she made sure nobody else would ever be able to reach her husband for the Lord.

How much more effective would have been the inside-the-family witnessing of this lady if she had followed the apostle Peter's advice and won her husband to the faith by her modest and blameless behavior. She was, indeed, a sweet woman with good character, a top-notch homemaker, and a highly talented artist. He probably could have been won to Jesus "without a word," for he could have found so much in her to admire. But the constant flood of preaching from her mouth stopped his ears and his heart to any message about the Lord.

Pearls to pigs is the metaphor Jesus chooses to warn us about trying to preach the Good News to those who don't want to hear it. Obviously Christ's focus in his sermon is broader than ours here. We're looking primarily at how this principle works in our families. But I am convinced that we can gain some important wisdom by applying our Lord's idea specifically to the knotty challenge of dealing lovingly and wisely with the unbelievers in our own homes.

**CHAPTER NINE**

# GOOD GIFTS FOR OUR CHILDREN

*Ask, and it will be given you; seek, and you will find; knock, and it will be opened to you. For every one who asks receives, and he who seeks finds, and to him who knocks it will be opened. Or what man of you, if his son asks him for bread, will give him a stone? Or if he asks for a fish, will give him a serpent? If you then, who are evil, know how to give good gifts to your children, how much more will your Father who is in heaven give good things to those who ask him!* (Matthew 7:7-11).

Some of us grew up in the Depression. Many of us were raised by parents who had known the tough times of the Depression. And then there are others among us—a younger generation—who think a depression is one reason to check into a mental hospital.

The Great Depression of the 20's and 30's left its mark on at least two generations—and possibly on three or four, depending on how you look at the matter. The impact of that time of hardship may explain most of what you are about to read in the next few pages.

To illustrate his teaching about prayer, Jesus said, "You who are evil know how to give good gifts to your children." Most of us who are near 65 or older were raised by parents who at that time did not have much to give us. The Depression had broken banks, bankrupted businesses, wiped out savings, and taken away jobs. It left a lot of families poor.

Jesus talked about fathers who gave their children gifts of bread and fish. Many Depression-time fathers felt fortunate if they could provide basic food like that for their families. More lavish gifts were out of the question.

During the years right after the Depression, my parents were smart gift-givers. Like most parents they wanted their kids to have packages under the Christmas tree, but they didn't have much money for such extras. So Mom wisely hoarded her purchases of necessary clothing items and wrapped them up as gifts for Christmas morning.

At least five Christmas mornings in a row I remember opening a package and finding in it a brand new pair of Levis—without patches on the knees! My, that was grand. Other packages always contained two or three sets of new undies and two or three pairs of socks. And always from our parents on those long-ago Christmases we received one single, inexpensive toy for each child.

As a kid I always thought I had a grand Christmas. I thought my parents gave good gifts to their children. I didn't even realize until I was grown that we got those specific gifts because we were poor folks.

**MORE THAN ENOUGH**

But those meager times passed. In an economy fueled by World War II, Americans became prosperous. The generation raised by Depression parents began to do well at work and in business. Is it a coincidence that their kids—the children of the troubled 60's—were the first generation raised by parents who had more than enough money to meet their needs?

I'm sure I would be grossly over-simplifying if I tried to trace all the troubles that shook America's homes in the 60's to our increased prosperity. Obviously more factors than just this one were at work. But if you lived through that time, I don't need to tell you that those were days that shook the longtime stable structures of American society.

My parents a decade earlier were concerned if I puffed on a filtered Viceroy. In the 60's parents trembled for the first time at the specter of teen-age drug abuse. Going to school was a privilege for my World War II generation. In the 60's we learned the term "drop-out" and applied it to thousands of mixed-up kids who bailed out of school several years early to "do their thing." We had social dropouts, too. We called them hippies or flower children, and—crazy as it may sound almost forty years later—for the most part those angry young people left posh upper-middle-class homes to go live in stinking communes with the over-educated unwashed.

At that time in our land families started falling apart as never before. Divorce rates soared and crime rates tried to keep pace. Race riots rocked our cities, and war protesters made the TV news almost every night. This was the era when theologians announced that "God is dead," and big-name reporters held weekly funerals for Christianity and for marriage and for traditional family lifestyles. Those were turbulent times.

At the high school where I teach the academic Bible course, hardly a week went by during the 1980's when I did not hear some teacher or administrator remark that the kids giving them headaches in school right then were the offspring of that mixed-up generation from the 60's. Thus they explained their students' confused hearts and minds. Today those same kids that often seemed so mixed up are running the school! And the White House!

Many forces were at work to derail that tragic 60's generation and, to some extent, the ones that have followed. But I am convinced that one of the strongest influences that unsettled our society was the unprecedented prosperity of most American families. A people raised in want suddenly emerged into a time of plenty. And we found ourselves in a game where we simply did not know the boundaries or the rules.

We knew how to run families that were poor.

Everybody worked hard.

Everybody did without some things.

Everybody helped everybody else.

And everybody behaved.

We could not afford to do otherwise.

But how do you handle a home when the bank account is growing monthly, and investments are beginning to pay off, and the family keeps needing a bigger house to hold all the new gadgets they are buying? Do you still expect the kids to work? Do you still expect everybody in the family to deny themselves "extras" and to "do without"?

Many good people who had it so hard in the Depression came out of it resolving that their children would never be deprived as they had been. They were like the parents Will Durant described in first-century Rome. "When the children came," Durant said, "they were loved not wisely but too well."

Jesus said, "You who are evil know how to give good gifts to your children." But not all of us do know how to do that. Many a child has been ruined because parents gave that child gifts that were *not* good.

**"TRAIN UP A CHILD"**

Two of the sharpest, sweetest people I know started off poor as

Job's proverbial turkey. Coming from impoverished homes, they struggled to pay for schooling during the Depression years. No wealthy parents were available to dole out dollars for tuition or for play. In the sparest of circumstances these good people began to raise a family, working hard and gradually rising above the poverty level of their early married days.

These are good people, the salt of the earth. All of their days they have been active leaders in their church and servants in their community. The man's company recognized his quality. He rose steadily from the lower ranks of the business to a high-paid role in the corporation's top leadership.

By the time their kids were in high school the family had moved to a fine house in a finer neighborhood. New cars filled their driveway. All the newest electronic equipment filled each child's bedroom. In other words, the kids had just about anything they wanted when they wanted it. This good man and woman lived to make sure that their kids would always have everything they needed (or, in actual fact, everything they asked for).

Today their three children have five or six divorces among them. I've lost count. Not only have they failed in marriage, they also have failed in every business they have attempted. One of the kids has been in serious trouble with the law.

My point is that all the efforts of these parents to launch their children with special blessings backfired. In trying to give their kids all the best advantages, they took away from them the greater advantage they themselves had enjoyed—the advantage of having to work hard for what they got. Letting their children grow up idle and unemployed, they took away from them the age-old training ground for responsibility and morals and values.

The Bible commands us, "Train up a child in the way he should go, and when he is old, he will not depart from it." No training in life skills and values remains in our culture for children whose parents simply give and give and give to their kids without expectations.

What would happen to a child if you never let him walk? If you loved him so much that you carried him everywhere and never let him endure the bumps and bruises that go with toddling, would he ever learn to stand alone or to take a step on his own? Would his leg muscles ever develop? Surely your love and your care for the child would make him a cripple.

What about the youngster who is never made to wait for what he wants, who is never made to save and struggle to obtain what he desires? What if we never require a child to work to get the big-ticket items most kids want today? His *legs* won't be crippled. His *values* will be weak and disabled. Possibly his value system will never even be formed.

Do you see what I am saying? By what we make too easily available, we can cripple our children. The gifts we give are not always good.

All of us in our age with its popular concern for the disadvantaged and the poor among us have seen how poverty devastates parenting and family-life skills. I know a family here in my town who just spent the last three months washing dishes in their bathtub. I know a lady who has not swept or vacuumed her house in over three years, and she lives with three dogs and two cats inside that filthy place. Poverty short-circuits the sort of day-to-day, how-to domestic knowledge most middle-class Americans take for granted.

But the truth is that prosperity may do just as much harm as poverty. No federal programs exist to take care of families whose children are clean and clothed and schooled—and godless.

## STONES AND SERPENTS

Several years ago our congregation reached back into decades past to show the original "Focus on the Family" video series by Dr. James Dobson. I can't quote Dr. Dobson precisely from memory, but I will never forget the gist of what he said about the training he wanted to give his children. In one of the films he spoke of the compelling burden he felt in his heart to raise children who would grow up in the faith, loving the Lord. And he said, "If they don't do that, I really don't care much what else they succeed in. If they don't grow up and live for the Lord, I don't care how much money they make."

I agree.

Jesus said, "If your son asks for bread, would you give him a stone? If he asks for a fish, would you give him a serpent?" The obvious answer is No. We would not knowingly give our children something so heartless and harmful.

Therein lies the tragedy. We never intend to damage our sons and daughters. But our deluded materialistic efforts to provide well for them have so often been their undoing. We *have* given our children a serpent if we have given them success without Christ. We *have* given them a stone if we have given them everything we had except our God.

I talked with a man some time ago, a man who in my opinion is an exceptionally smart man. By the time he was 40 he had risen to the top in his profession. In a large city he had one of the best jobs. It had prestige. It paid well. Right at the pinnacle of his career, he quit. He moved from Miami to a small town out in the sticks in Ohio to a nothing-job at less than half the former salary.

"Why are you doing this?" his shocked colleagues and friends screamed.

"I need to spend time with my boys," he explained simply. "I need to give my sons what I can never give them with the big job and the big salary. I need to give them my faith and my values and my Lord."

This man knew how to give good gifts to his children.

**CHAPTER TEN**

# THE GOLDEN RULE

*So whatever you wish that men would do to you, do so to them; for this is the law and the prophets* (Matthew 7:6).

Shattered beer bottles, discarded soft drink cans, assorted food wrappers, and crumpled sacks with fast-food logos litter the Interstate highway median of I-27 every weekend morning. Just from looking at the accumulated debris at sunrise on Sunday it is hard to tell whether to blame the mess on the previous night's stream of thoughtless students going to and from the nearby university or whether the residents of the trailer house ghetto along the highway have mindlessly trashed their own neighborhood. But it's a cinch that somebody in the area keeps making a huge mess that seems to get worse with each passing year.

Am I jumping to an unwarranted conclusion when I suggest that Christians who live by the Lord's famous Golden Rule don't behave this way?

Because I do not enjoy picking up some oaf's discarded trash, I don't toss out my garbage in public places where somebody else will have to pick it up. Neither do you, if you are trying to live by the Golden Rule.

So I have a theory that the growing tendency to trash America may be an indicator that the practical influence of Christianity is waning with the passing of each generation. The sort of selfishness that allows one human to blithely ignore another person's rights and well-being is basically unChristian—the opposite of the Golden Rule.

Pull onto the crowded parking lot of any busy supermarket on Saturday afternoon and you can observe the same phenomenon. Most of the customers have been careful to take only one space, but when the lot is packed and spaces are hard to find, invariably some clod has inconsiderately straddled a line and used up two spaces.

Am I right again that this sort of disdain for the welfare of others is the opposite of the Christian attitude that always tries to treat others as thoughtfully as we want to be treated?

Maybe the offender is a good Christian but a lousy driver. I always hope so. But the selfishness that takes no thought of all the others who are trying to park seems again to be a growing spirit—one that might seem to signal in this setting also a decline in the number of citizens who shape their behavior by the Golden Rule.

My wife and I enjoyed a quiet lunch together today. It was an hour worth remembering because it was the first time in ages that we have dined in a restaurant without having somebody's unruly child ruin the experience for us.

Nita and I like kids. Most of the time at home and at church we are surrounded by them, and we love it. What we don't like is the selfishness of a growing number of young parents who seem to be oblivious to the fact that the ruckus being raised by their child is ruining the meal for a whole dining room full of people.

Common sense—as well as Golden Rule sensitivity—would seem to dictate that a mother or father either quiet the troubled child quickly or take the little howler outside. Thoughtful people still do it that way. But we rarely eat a meal in a café these days without some family allowing their offspring to ruin the occasion for everybody there.

Is this another example that Christian influence on our society is shrinking as fewer and fewer people are concerned to treat others the way they would like to treated?

Let me confess to you that I may be way out in left field on this premise that selfishness indicates a lack of commitment to Christ.

People who appear to be selfish in their behavior may just be addled. The unconscious souls who block supermarket aisles and those who dawdle in rush-hour traffic may turn out to be loving, kind, Christ-honoring folks who are just out to lunch. (If this is true, it would appear that the mushrooming rates of muddleheadedness call for quick and close attention from the folks at the Mental Health/Mental Retardation office.)

Maybe the problem involves some of both factors—we have some neighbors who are simply out of it at the moment, and we have a host of other folks who are callously, cussedly selfish.

I have the latter group in my crosshairs right now. These are the folks who appear to have no intention of practicing our Lord's simple, practical Rule for respecting the rest of us who must live alongside them in this world. By their selfishness they send a clear message that Christ's way is not their way.

**ALL IN THE FAMILY**

Where are we most likely to learn to follow the Golden Rule?

In the modern age with our schools and textbooks so carefully sanitized of all references to God, Christ, the church, or morality, we probably won't hear about the Golden Rule in school. Hopefully, we might see genuine Christian unselfishness modeled by Christian teachers, but they can't legally tell us why they have chosen to respect the feelings and preferences of the people around them.

If we are churchgoing people, chances are good that we will both hear and see the Golden Rule as it is taught in our sermons and Bible studies and as it is practiced by those devout souls in the church who are serious about doing things Christ's way. And that's good as far as it goes.

Would you agree with me, though, that Christ's Golden Rule has by far its strongest impact on our behavior as we see it demonstrated in the daily actions of our parents? Without even knowing it, as we watch our Christian parents we are learning this wise way to get along with other people.

- If your kids see you slow down to allow a bottled-up car to merge into a long line of traffic, what have they learned from you?
- We live in a time-conscious world where most of us constantly race against a clock. Do your children see you taking special care not to needlessly delay others on a sidewalk, at the supermarket checkout counter, or in the usual long line at the post office?
- When it's time to pay for your purchases, do you speed up things by having your check made out or your money in hand so the line behind you has less time to wait? Do you behave the way you would like for them to if they were ahead of you?
- Do you insist that your family be as careful of your neighbor's property as you want his kids and pets to be of yours?

- If you smoke, are you careful not to let your nasty habit annoy others? (The other day I saw a sign that said, "If you won't blow your smoke in my face, I won't spit my tobacco on your boots." Is that a crude statement of the Golden Rule?)
- Golden Rule folks obviously take care not to disturb their neighborhood with wild parties or loud music. They don't mow their lawn at 7 a.m. on Saturday when half the neighbors are trying to sleep in.
- Do you speak to your children in the same tone of voice you would prefer for them to use if they were your parent?
- Are you as truthful to them as you expect them to be to you? How much does the Golden Rule shape the closest relationships in your family?

A list like this obviously could run on and on. I hope this is sufficient to drive home my point that most of us will grow up to treat other people about like our parents did. If Mom and Dad are Golden Rule keepers, the kids usually will reflect this kind of respect and care for others.

## A SPIRITUAL EQUATION

So the most crucial training ground for Golden Rule living appears to be the home. I can't think of a finer legacy to leave to our children, and to their children. For the math students among us, however, let me suggest that a spiritual equation can be devised to measure the operative force of Christ's great Rule: *A family's practice of the Golden Rule will be in direct proportion to their honor for Christ.*

The equation works in four stages:

*Stage 1*—The full force of the Golden Rule will be at work in a Christian home where all members of the family love the Lord and live by his word. The way they relate to one another and the way they treat other people generally will reflect the Rule. And it is a beautiful thing to behold. When you know that every other person in your family intends to show you the same love and fairness and honesty they want from you, you are set free from the jealousy and distrust and bitterness that mar so many homes. What a blessing to be part of a Golden Rule family! What a privilege it is to deal with a family like that! This is the Golden Rule full force, at its best.

*Stage 2*—This is a home where the parents are Christians who try to live by the Golden Rule, but the kids in this home stray from their parents' faith. They give up church for the good life. They may replace worship and Bible study with a non-stop schedule of work and play. Usually these non-church-going kids will continue to reflect the Golden Rule in the way they treat people at school, on the ball field, or on the job. In their personal relationships they will tend to imitate the Christian parents who raised them. But something will be missing. Without faith in the Lord who gave the Golden Rule, this generation will go through the motions without understanding why. The Rule without the Christ who gave it cannot long survive.

*Stage 3*—Now we have a home where kids are being raised by parents who probably are decent people, but Christ and the church have no place in their lives. Without knowing it, the parents in this stage still may practice the Golden Rule most of the time as they mindlessly mimic their own parents and grandparents. But the children raised in this Stage 3 home have no memories of Christian faith. They never knew the godly great-grandparents who embodied the Lord's Golden Rule. So at this stage pagan selfishness likely will replace Christian love as the motivating force in their relationships both inside and outside the home.

*Stage 4*—By the time we reach this stage, where all honor for Christ has been lost in the home, the Golden Rule usually vanishes, too. The parents now produce a houseful of heathens—selfish to the core—who abuse one another and become a burden to society because they are concerned for nobody's pleasure but their own.

Rapidly growing in our land, this is the set of citizens I described at the beginning of this chapter. These are the hooligans who litter the freeway with their throwaways. These are the in-your-face oafs who don't care if anybody else gets a parking place. These are the selfish souls who don't care whose dinner they ruin as long as they enjoy theirs. Ignorant of the Golden Rule and disdainful of such religious weakness, they tend to be devoid of the gentleness and goodness modeled by Jesus. Many of them have exchanged his Golden Rule for the rule of gold.

Ours is not the first generation where this has happened. Judges 2:7-12 tells us:
*And the people served the Lord all the days of Joshua, and all the days of the elders who outlived Joshua, who had seen all the great work which the Lord had done for Israel . . . And all that generation also were gathered to their fathers; and there arose another generation after them, who did not know the Lord or the work which he had done for Israel. And the people of Israel did what was evil in the sight of the Lord and served the Ba'als; and they forsook the Lord, the God of their fathers.*

My random observations of our present practice of something as basic and simple as the Golden Rule convinces me that in America we are working through similar stages today, with a large segment of our population moving from devout faith, to imitation faith, and finally to no faith at all. As a larger segment of our society abandons any vestige of Christian faith, public behavior shows it.

**WITH OR WITHOUT JESUS**

Does this explain the precipitant loss of integrity in top finance circles in our land? We used to trust corporate leaders to protect the best interests of their investors. Then Enron came along. We used to trust certified auditors to keep companies like Enron honest. Then Arthur Andersen started shredding company records. Now many investors wonder if they can trust the financial records of any American corporation.

Could a debacle like this have occurred if the main players in the business world still adhered to basic Christian principles of truth and honesty? Or is this a glimpse of what we can look forward to as the unchurched flower-child generation rises to positions of leadership in our land?

Despite valid constitutional concerns about the relationship of church and state, we are learning the hard way in America that loss of faith translates into major changes in the way the people in our nation behave.

In this chapter I started off by focusing attention on everyday selfishness that shows an absence of Golden Rule mentality. If the present trends in this area continue, we're in for some rude, crude times. In a national survey taken early in 2002, 79 percent of those interviewed said they were experiencing a rising level of rudeness in their daily lives. That's sad. But the waning of Christian faith in our nation opens the way for far more serious behavioral shifts.

At the risk of sounding petty, I chose at the beginning of this chapter to illustrate my point with trivial offenses such as shameless littering and inconsiderate parking and high-decibel dining. But our loss of faith has far more serious implications. Just how much our faith (or lack thereof) determines the quality of life for all of us becomes starkly apparent from even a brief review of our nation's worst social problems. As more and more Americans jettison Christianity, it is not just the Golden Rule they leave behind.

Drugs began to blight America's black neighborhoods right at the time when young blacks began to abandon the churches that had been so important to their grandparents. Today young black males have the shortest life expectancy of any group in the U.S.

Crack babies were an inevitable result of rampant drug addiction. Studies show that most of them are born to mothers who are three generations removed from active Christian faith.

If you are a radical Muslim, you know that the sexual content of American television and the Internet are unacceptable by any religious standard of purity. But an alarming number of Americans no longer seem to know this. As we drift farther from our Christian roots, instances of pornography addiction, promiscuity, sexual deviancy, and sex abuse climb to record levels.

Those who turn their backs on Jesus and scoff at his instructions for righteous living unknowingly verify his own observation. In the Sermon on the Mount he predicts that those who reject his "narrow way" will find themselves on a path that leads to destruction. Far too many of our contemporaries have chosen that road.

In its familiar shortened form, our Lord's rule that his followers call "golden" says, "Do unto others what you would have them do unto you." Don't let the Rule's simplicity fool you. The Golden Rule is not a Sunday school lesson given only to amuse children. It is not a stained-glass platitude to be intoned with pastoral piety on Sunday but then dismissed as hopelessly impractical on Monday. Our willingness to live by the Golden Rule is one unmistakable sign that we truly belong to Jesus.

**CHAPTER ELEVEN**

# THE NARROW WAY

*Enter by the narrow gate; for the gate is wide and the way is easy, that leads to destruction, and those who enter by it are many. For the gate is narrow and the way is hard, that leads to life, and those who find it are few* (Matthew 7:13-14).

I began preaching before I began shaving. Most of the congregations who suffered through my fledgling sermons were small rural churches who must have been the most lovable, patient people in the word. Some of them let me practice on them for years.

When I say "small" churches, I mean really small. Some of them did good to turn up a baker's dozen on Sunday morning. But they were fine, sweet folks who treated me kindly and never once even hinted that I did not yet know how to preach. Many of them have been important people in my life for more than fifty years.

In those tiny congregations I first heard Jesus' words about the narrow gate being used in a way he surely did not intend them. Several times during those years I heard some good brother imply to the assembled worshipers that we should not despair that we were so few, for Jesus said of the true way, "*Few* there be that find it."

Nobody ever challenged this distortion of Scripture. Instead we found an odd sort of comfort in our "fewness." The fact that we were so "few" seemed somehow to be God's seal of approval on our way of "doing church."

Hundreds of other believers were worshiping at the same hour in those tiny communities, but of all the people in town, we were convinced that we alone were right. We were the ones who had found the way that leads to life. If you doubted that, it could be easily verified by the fact that we were the smallest church in town. We were few. And you know what Jesus said about the "few."

It never dawned on us to read Acts 2 at just that moment. There we could have learned that the Jerusalem church was born 3,000 members strong. Surely those people baptized by the apostles themselves had found the right way—the narrow way, and they certainly were not few by our standards. But we chose not to notice passages like that. It was much more soothing to our souls to explain our smallness as a sign of our goodness.

We did have one thing right. It is for sure that we were on a narrow way—a *very* narrow way. In many respects it probably was not the one Jesus had in mind in his sermon, but nobody could deny that the path we had chosen to walk in the name of Christ was narrow.

## NARROW IS NOT ENOUGH

Let me offer three brief observations about the narrow way.

The first one should be quickly apparent to us: *Some of the narrowest roads people walk on still lead to destruction.* It is not enough for us to choose a road that is narrow. What appear to be very narrow tracks may turn out to be well-disguised ruts in that broader way Jesus warns us about.

Years ago I knew an active church family whose lifestyle was the narrowest of the narrow. (To protect identities, I will change the facts here slightly, but the basic ingredients of this tale are true ones that well illustrate my point.)

These parents were super-strict with their children. And they were "churchy," even at home. Just as some preachers have a pulpit voice, these folks had a "church voice" which showed up whenever they needed to demonstrate how right and holy they were in some judgment. To their adult friends I suppose they sounded holy and pious and syrupy sweet. To my irreverent juvenile ears they sounded as false as the witch in Walt Disney's *Snow White*.

In later years I found that my childish ears had heard it right. I have never observed fiercer anger in any clan. Especially toward one another they were hostile. The kids grew up and their marriages fell apart one by one. Members of the family became alienated from one another.

I mention all this, not to judge these unhappy people, but to illustrate my point. They walked an extraordinarily narrow religious road. But I say to you that a road broad enough to contain hateful anger and bitter hostility between loved ones is a road that leads to destruction—regardless of how narrow it seems to be.

In another time and place I knew a sweet Christian lady whose life was so narrow that she refused to take part in most of the things normal Christians enjoy. The watchword of her life was stern self-denial. We should not criticize her for this, of course. It was her privilege to choose such a disciplined life if it helped her draw nearer to the Lord.

But she was also afraid. She was afraid of public schools. She was afraid of government at almost every level. She was afraid of ordinary things most informed Christians accept without a flicker.

Privately I always suspected that this lady would have been glad to join John the Baptist in the wilderness far away from the contaminations of daily living. But, if she had, I'm sure she would have given the prophet fits for indulging in all that honey.

I have no way to know for certain what motivated this lady to choose such a narrow approach to life. Only God knows, and he alone will be her judge. For the sake of illustration, however, let us suppose that her narrowness resulted not from true righteousness in her soul, but from a deep fear of living and from envy toward those who had things she never would have and toward those who were allowed to do things she never could do.

A road broad enough to allow us to haul along a load of fear and envy is not the narrow road that leads to life, is it?

The world is full of people who walk on narrow roads. Who could be narrower than a Nazi? To him only people with blonde hair and blue eyes are acceptable. That's narrow!

The Ku Klux Klan espouses a similarly narrow view. Only white people are loved by God, they believe. I wonder if they realize what a small percentage of the people on our globe are pale skinned.

For narrowness and meanness, nobody could out-hate some of the radical feminist leaders of the decades just past. They make Christians who preach sectarian hatred appear to be full of love and grace.

And, of course, in more recent tragic days we have seen the sickening display of the narrow maliciousness of those renegade Muslims who call themselves Taliban. Is there anybody they don't hate?

People like these walk extremely exclusive paths. Their roads are open only to the faithful few. They hold a patent on narrowness. But I insist that a road broad enough to accommodate a heart full of hatred for most of mankind is too broad to please our Lord.

## THE MAJORITY CHOICE

A second observation: *Because the broad way is chosen by the majority, it will almost always look like the more acceptable way.* When we opt for the narrower path, our associates usually wonder about us. They raise their eyebrows and suppose out loud that we must be some sort of nut. To describe us, they may mutter the word "fanatic." Because of our basic human need for approval, it's hard to be the target for that sort of evaluation.

For this reason alone, if for no other, the efforts to curtail drug abuse in America are failing. An insecure 15-year-old kid surrounded by older buddies who are shooting up or smoking grass finds it almost impossible to refuse to join the crowd and thus risk their ridicule. "Everybody else is doing it" has for ages been the teen-age description of the broad way.

And it's not just the misguided teen who wavers before the mob. Even as a seasoned preacher I find it hard to voice what sounds like an unpopular heresy to our modern generation of suburban dwellers—the urgent truth that as young parents they ought to insist that school and community programs leave their kids alone at least part of the time so they can enjoy some quality family time.

This message raises the hackles of Little League coaches and high school band directors. A fellow who says much about it in public will soon be labeled a spoilsport and a troublemaker. But some of us need to tell our school officials and our community sports programmers that kids who are too busy to spend one evening a week with their parents are too busy.

Please don't mistake my real concern here. I see nothing wrong with high school extra-curricular activities or with Little League ball. My kids participated. I coached. But I know now that I made a mistake when I failed to demand equal time for our family to be together. School and community activities took my kids away from me at the age when I could have enjoyed them the most (and, possibly, when my presence might have benefited them the most). And I didn't have the guts or the brains to make the unpopular noises that might have changed things.

The broad, majority-rule way seems so reasonable and right to the majority. God have mercy on the poor bloke who speaks a very loud word against it!

Churches with an active singles program know what I am talking about. The broad, popular line today sees nothing at all wrong with single folks sleeping together. In fact, our society hints that something might be a bit strange about the single who does not find a sexual outlet.

Talk to the minister of any church with a large singles program and you will talk to a Christian who is going through some gut-wrenching about how to accept what he knows is going on and still stand for the scriptural truths about fornication. If he calls insistently for the narrow way of the Lord, which specifies sex in marriage only, he will say good-bye to many of his single members. The narrow way seldom seems reasonable or acceptable.

Jesus was right, wasn't he? The way that leads to life is lonesome and hard.

### THE RIGHT DESTINATION

Observation number three: *The narrow way may not make us popular, but it does lead to life.*

How many people have you known who said, "I'm not going to be tied down by a bunch of religious rules. I'm going to *live*"? They set out down the broad way looking for what they call "the good life." Too late they find out that "you can't get there from here." The broad, easy way does not lead to life.

Satan's oldest lie implies that God with all his rules is just trying to keep us from enjoying what we really could have in life if we were not so hung up. He used that pitch on Adam and Eve in Eden: "There's really nothing wrong with that fruit. God just wants to keep you from realizing all your possibilities. Come on, Babe, have a bite!"

When we buy Satan's line, we have bought a one-way ticket to death. It was that way in the garden. It is that way today.

I remember the commercials actor Yul Brynner made right before lung cancer asphyxiated him. For three decades he fouled his lungs with enormous quantities of burnt nicotine. Too late he discovered what he had done to extinguish his marvelous talents and to cut short his prime-of-life days. "Don't come this way!" he warned in a raspy, dying voice. "This way leads to destruction."

The broad way always does.

## THE BIG QUESTION

And now—the most important question of all. How can Christian parents raise kids who will always choose the narrow way?

Honesty dictates an immediate answer. They can't. Their kids are human beings, not angels. Parents of human children cannot positively assure that their kids will always choose for God and for good, not any more than the Creator could have a guarantee that Adam and Eve would always choose the right way.

Having recognized that our children will fail at times and that they will be just as dependent on God's grace as we their parents have been, we still face the question of how we can aim our children toward the narrow way that leads to life.

No sure-fire answers exist, but I offer these suggestions.

First of all, nothing will shape our children's choices in life more than our own choices. If we consistently choose the narrow way, if we opt for the Lord and for life, our offspring are likely to follow our path.

If they see us often abusing alcohol, or if they see their middle-aged daddy chasing skirts, we can be fairly sure that their lifestyle will not be much different.

You and I cannot make our children's choices when they are grown and gone from home, but we can influence their choices every day of their lives by always choosing the narrow way ourselves.

A second suggestion. Be sure that your kids leave home not with your faith but with their own. We can't follow our grown kids around to wipe their moral noses and to make all their choices for them, but we don't have to if they take the Lord with them wherever they go.

A third, highly important tack: choose your kid's friends carefully. If your child runs with a group that honors Christ, she probably will, too. If your son's or daughter's friends are cruising down the broad way of life, your child will likely follow them to destruction. We are seldom much better than the friends we spend our time with, whether we are young or old.

Refuse to allow your child to spend long, unsupervised hours with kids who are no-good. Make it hard for your son or daughter to associate with the crowd that drinks and does drugs but never does church. Choosing friends walking on the right road makes as much sense as choosing a bus traveling the right highway. You can't get to the right place on the wrong road.

The narrow way, which seems so barren and stern and hard, leads finally to life. But it takes a wise person to see that, and most folks won't. Very few people take the right road. That's what Jesus said.

*"Enter by the narrow gate; for the gate is wide and the way is easy that leads to destruction, and those who enter by it are many. For the gate is narrow and the way is hard, that leads to life, and those who find it are few."*

**CHAPTER TWELVE**

# FALSE PROPHETS TO FAMILIES

*Beware of false prophets, who come to you in sheep's clothing but inwardly are ravenous wolves. You will know them by their fruits. Are grapes gathered from thorns, or figs from thistles? So, every sound tree bears good fruit, but the bad tree bears evil fruit. A sound tree cannot bear evil fruit, nor can a bad tree bear good fruit. Every tree that does not bear good fruit is cut down and thrown into the fire. Thus you will know them by their fruits.*

*Not every one who says to me, "Lord, Lord," shall enter the kingdom of heaven, but he who does the will of my Father who is in heaven. On that day many will say to me, "Lord, Lord, did we not prophesy in your name, and cast out demons in your name, and do many mighty works in your name?" And then will I declare to them, "I never knew you; depart from me, you evildoers"* (Matthew 7:15-23).

The school board in Provincetown, Mass., decided that their preschoolers needed to know more about homosexuality. So, according to the Washington *Times* (Aug. 21, 1997), they set up an arrangement for a group called Parents, Families, and Friends of Lesbians and Gays to speak in their kindergarten classes.

At Pleasant Valley School in Marin County, Calif., all the second-through-fifth graders were subjected to an assembly that featured a local theater group. The students were taught slogans such as "I'm gay and it's O.K." *Citizen* magazine (July 2001) reported that one of the third-grade girls came home from school that day and asked her father, "Am I a lesbian?" She thought she might be, since she liked girls better than boys.

In the spring of 2001, Focus on the Family warned on their web site that the National Education Association was planning to vote soon on a resolution to implement "pro-homosexual curricula, instructional materials, programs, and hiring of homosexual educators in America's public schools." According to this article, NEA was keeping this move under wraps, but it came as no surprise, since the leaders of NEA, such as then-president Bob Chase, have been outspoken about their pro-homosexual agenda for our public schools.

"Watch out for false prophets," Jesus warns us in the Sermon on the Mount. Over and over the Bible echoes this warning about those who would mislead God's people in matters of faith and morals. Since our focus for the moment is on the Lord's wisdom for our families, let's confine this False-Prophet Alert at least for now to a call for vigilance against those who would pervert the Lord's will for Christian homes.

If you watch much television, listen to talk radio, or read the popular magazines of our day, do I have to tell you that our age has produced a host of false prophets for families?

As Jesus warns in this part of his famous sermon, these anti-family advocates wear sheep's clothing. To give credibility to the domestic nonsense they dump on us daily, some of them parade on TV as hosts of big-name, prime-time shows, or they try to dazzle us with their impressive academic degrees.

These false family prophets often boast that, unlike the pastor in the pulpit down the street, *they* are politically correct. And, just as Jesus warns in his Sermon, some of the false prophets try to gain an audience by crying, "Lord, Lord!" They flaunt prestigious religious credentials to justify their off-the-wall theories of child rearing, or marital arrangements, or sexual deviancy.

And, as you would expect, our Lord's analysis proves true, for the fruit produced by the message of these false prophets turns out to be broken homes, broken lives, broken hearts, broken promises. This "tree" surely cannot be any good because its fruit is rotten to the core.

### WHO ARE THEY?

Just who are these false prophets Jesus warns us about? How can we recognize them and their pernicious theories? It's not hard. If we have even the most basic awareness of right and wrong, good and evil, moral and immoral as set forth in God's word, we should not have any trouble recognizing these false teachers. At the risk of making this chapter more negative than I want to, let me unmask a few of them.

*Planned Parenthood*

High on any list of those who distort Christian family values must be the group known as Planned Parenthood. In his book, *The Myths of Sex Education*, Josh McDowell exposes Planned Parenthood's spurious claim that their sex education materials are morally neutral.

In their unit on "Boys and Sex," for instance, Planned Parenthood tells our school children, "Premarital intercourse does have its definite value as a training ground for marriage or some other committed relationships. . . . It's like taking a car out on a test run before you buy it."

In Planned Parenthood's material called "Girls and Sex," students are told that many girls will later regret not having had sex before marriage "because they've come to realize what a long, slow learning process it can often be after marriage."

That's a far cry from what Jesus tells us, isn't it? In a list of "evil thoughts, murder, adultery, theft, false witness, and slander," Jesus includes fornication. He says it defiles a person and makes them unclean (Matthew 15:19-20). But Planned Parenthood says it will make you feel better about yourself and improve your marriage.

How hard is it to identify the false prophet here?

The Bible calls fornication a "work of the flesh"—along with things like idolatry, sorcery, drunkenness, and carousing—and it teaches plainly that "those who do such things shall not inherit the kingdom of God" (Galatians 5:19-21).

Planned Parenthood tells our sons and daughters that sex before marriage is the normal, smart thing to do. Even in their sheep's clothing of government-awarded educational contracts, the false prophet is not hard to spot.

*Family Professionals*

We have to be careful in this area, because many family professionals with impressive credentials are giving out bad advice.

Missionary Jim Albright got defensive for his native friends in Malawi when he saw a paper that was circulated all across that nation on a recent Valentine's Day. Using your tax dollars and mine, the medical team charged with controlling AIDS in that small nation told their people that while sexual abstinence and marital fidelity are good, for "most Malawians" such ideals are "impossible." This made Jim mad. "What a patronizing statement!" he snorted. And he's right, whether you say it about Malawi villagers or about American teenagers.

Here at home in America some marriage and family counselors belong on the False Prophet list. Despite their long years of training and their expertise in helping clients deal with crises in their lives, many professional psychologists and counselors disdain Christian family values and therefore advise their patients to find happiness by violating God's commands.

Even when the adjective "Christian" is used to define the counselor, we can't always be sure that the counsel being given reflects Christ's teachings on family matters.

Several years ago in Fort Worth a Christian couple trying to weather a mid-life crisis sought the services of a well-known "Christian counselor." After several sessions, the professional told the wife that her husband was an immature flake and that she deserved someone better. He told her she needed to get a divorce and get on with her life.

This unhappy woman ignored what Jesus says about divorce and followed her counselor's advice.

God says, "I hate divorce." So do most people who have been through one. Counselors who see divorce as the quickest, least painful, and therefore the preferred solution to most marital discord need to line up for their "False Prophet" badges.

It's not just the counselors who ignore God. Sometimes physicians do, too. Several years ago on one large Texas campus the university's physician responded in the daily campus newspaper to questions about sexually transmitted diseases. She wrote that sexual abstinence is admirable, but "we can't realistically expect our young people to practice it."

In a letter to the editor of the school newspaper, a Christian professor at the school called the doctor's statement "irresponsible." He assured her that millions of people of faith have abstained from sex before marriage. "Abstinence is a most realistic course for those with moral and religious conviction," he wrote. "It is a small price to pay to avoid the misery and other consequences of promiscuity."

The campus doctor admitted later that her remark had been "a bit careless." A bit? An STD prevention official condoning sex on a busy college campus is not a whole lot different from a kindergarten supervisor handing out loaded pistols for the kids to play with at recess. Somebody's gonna get hurt.

*Media Gurus*

From Oprah or Geraldo to Jerry Springer or Sally Jesse Raphael we hear all sorts of advice about how to lead our lives and run our families, much of that advice coming from losers recruited to appear on these shows precisely because their life choices have been so bizarre. False prophets for families seem these days to be America's favorite media darlings.

False prophets use newsprint as well as TV screens. In her Sept. 28, 2001, column, nationally syndicated columnist Ann Landers responded to a mother who was concerned that her 20-year-old college student daughter was involved in a lesbian relationship. "If your daughter is lesbian, be aware this is not something she chose. She was born to be attracted to members of her own sex. It's the way she is emotionally 'wired,'" Landers told the troubled mother. "I urge you to accept her partner with grace and hope other family members will as well."

Landers didn't make up this description of lesbianism, of course. In the past two decades gay and lesbian activists have successfully sold this as the politically correct view of homosexuality. "We're born this way," they insist. "We're just being ourselves." But God's word tells us that lesbianism is "unnatural"—the product of "shameful lusts" (Romans 1:26).

A local columnist in the Abilene, Texas *Reporter*, Laurie Abbo, has written several books for families, including one called *The Ten Commandments of Holistic Parenting*. In one of her columns she advised a girl's parents to allow their daughter to embrace Wicca and not to stifle her with objections. Wicca is probably a lot like Christianity anyway, Abbo wrote, showing how little she evidently knows about either religion.

Wicca is not the only evil Ms. Abbo is uninformed about. In her July 24, 1999, column she told a concerned mother that in her opinion it is "very healthy and extremely normal" for a 15-year-old boy to be dabbling in pornography. She said, "I would be more concerned if my son had no interest in these things."

Journalistic objectivity is a laudable trait in a reporter. Moral oblivion is not. We expect the average five-year-old to know the difference between right and wrong, between what is allowable and what is not. Unfortunately, this expert on family life flunked the kindergarten test on morality. I don't think Abbo intends to mislead her readers, but the advice she gives them can ruin their lives and damn their souls.

*Religious Leaders*

"False prophets" Jesus warns us to watch for. And in matters pertaining to our families they seem to be everywhere, even in the highest ranks of church leadership.

Do you realize that in the last half of the 20th century it was liberal church leaders who led the movements to liberalize divorce laws and to legalize abortions? During the past decade top officials in several Christian denominations have made headlines with their defiant support for the ordination of homosexuals and for their churches' approval of same-sex "marriages."

To the shame of all Christians, clerics with impressive credentials have led the social assault on biblical norms for family relationships.

And it is not just the church bigwigs who are guilty of perverting God's rules for the home. When the lay elders in a conservative church in Phoenix, Arizona, recently discovered that a deacon candidate's wife had been divorced, they ruled that the couple could not please God unless they divorced and the woman remarried her first husband. The way to cure a divorce, according to these addled church shepherds, is to get another divorce. Got that?

A colleague of mine recalls a time in his childhood church when a visiting preacher stridently proclaimed that since God will not forgive those who have not confessed their sins and repented of them, then God does not expect any of us to forgive an offending family member until that person repents and asks for our forgiveness. According to this spokesman for the Lord, bearing a grudge against an impenitent parent or sibling is the holy, god-like thing to do.

False prophets.

Watch out for them, Jesus warns us.

It can be confusing, because not all of them are advocating immorality. Tom Peters and Nancy Austin are management trainers who preach corporate excellence. They have been dismayed to see how many good people "on the way to the top" have bought into the ruinous philosophy that in order to succeed they must give up family vacations, Little League, birthday dinners, family meal times, and any domestic leisure pursuits such as gardening, reading, going to movies, or enjoying hobbies.

The result of such mixed-up priorities has been an epidemic of failed marriages for these rising executives. Peters and Austin confess, "There are more newly single parents than we expected among our colleagues."

To return to our Lord's analogy, the fruit of the false teachers turns out to be rancid and bitter. "By their fruit you shall know them."

## THE PROPHET WHOSE MESSAGE IS TRUE

If this has been dismal so far, wash out your ears and refresh your soul with this story told by our present United States Attorney General John Ashcroft. It's a true story about his own godly father.

Quoted from Ashcroft's book, *Lessons from a Father to His Son*, this poignant tale demonstrates the strength and goodness that can result when genuine Christian values undergird our homes. Ashcroft calls the story "Struggling To Kneel."

*Though we all enjoy the brilliant array of colors in the fall, few of us understand the process that changes a tree's colors. As the hours of sunlight grow shorter, the tree produces less green chlorophyll. As the green of this natural chemical departs from the trees, the leaves are finally able to reveal their natural color. It's not until the chlorophyll runs out in the fall that the true glory of nature's spectacular colors is visible.*

*Much like a mighty tree, my dad's true colors were the most vivid at the end of his life. When he had just hours left to live, I truly saw my father at his brightest, clearest, and finest. It was a day I will never forget.*

*THE SPIRIT OF WASHINGTON*

*Before each of my inaugurations as governor, I asked that there be a special time where friends and officials would join together to invite the presence of God both in the inaugural festivities and in the administration I would direct. In a personal and public way, I wanted to signal my individual dependence on God and our corporate dependence on the mercy of the Almighty. In 1985 and 1989, Missourians from all walks of life and every corner of the state attended these services of consecration and dedication.*

*The night before I was sworn in to the Senate in 1995, my father arranged for some close friends and family—maybe fifteen to twenty people—to gather for dinner. My father eyed a piano in the corner of the room and said, "John, why don't you play the piano and we'll sing?"*

*"Okay, Dad. You name it, I'll play it."*

*"Let's sing, 'We Are Standing on Holy Ground.'"*

*It was one of my father's favorites, but he was not engaging in some sentimental ploy by suggesting it. As I would later learn, a profound purpose undergirded his request.*

*After the song, I eased away from the piano keys and found myself thinking out loud. "We're standing here having a good time," I said, "but I really wish we were in a dedication service."*

*The impending responsibilities of the Senate were already weighing heavily upon me. I did not have an inflated view of my importance as a senator, but I was not lackadaisical about it either. The people of Missouri had sent me to the Senate to represent them, and I wanted to do so with integrity and character.*

*My lifelong friend, Dick Foth, spoke up. "We can do something about a dedication service, John."*

*At Dick's suggestion, we gathered early the next morning at a house not far from the Capitol. It was a beautiful house, decorated in Early American style, and maintained by a group of friends for the express purpose of bringing members of Congress together for spiritual enrichment.*

*We began by chatting informally and then sang a hymn or two. At the time ! did not realize how weak my father was, but he had been losing weight through the months of November and December and had told an acquaintance of his, "I'm hanging on by a thread, and it's a thin thread at that, but I'm going to see John sworn into the Senate."*

*As we talked, the earnestness of my father's voice suddenly commanded everyone's attention. "John," Dad said, "please listen carefully." My children and I fixed our focus on Dad. My brother Bob moved to the edge of his seat. Dick Foth and the others leaned in.*

*"The spirit of Washington is arrogance," my dad said, "and the spirit of Christ is humility. Put on the spirit of Christ. Nothing of lasting value has ever been accomplished in arrogance."*

*The room was absolutely quiet. All of us were absorbed by what my father had said, and we awaited what he was struggling to say next.*

*"Someday I hope that someone will come up to you as you're fulfilling your duties as a senator, tug on your sleeve, and say, 'Senator, your spirit is showing.'"*

*There could be no more lighthearted banter after that. We were living a truly profound moment.*

*Back when I was eight years old, my father had used a breathtaking dive in an old Piper Cub to convince me that my actions had great consequence; now, nearly half a century later, he wanted me to remember that how I did what I did would have eternal impact.*

*After we discussed my father's words, I finally asked that we have a time of solemn prayer.*

*The ancient kings of Israel, David and Saul, were anointed as they undertook their administrative duties, as were some leaders in the early church. My denomination frequently follows this practice. Accordingly, I was anointed prior to each of my terms as governor.*

*"It's too bad we don't have any oil," I said.*

*"Let's see if there's something in the kitchen," my father suggested.*

*Dick Foth disappeared to the kitchen where Janet Potter gave him a tiny bowl of Crisco oil. We chuckled about that, but my father assured us, "The oil itself isn't important, except as a symbol of the spirit of God."*

*I knelt in front of the sofa where my father was seated, and everyone gathered around me. Most placed a hand on my head, shoulders, or back. Everyone was standing when I noticed my father lunging, swinging his arms, trying to lift himself out of the couch, one of those all-enveloping pieces of furniture that tends to bury you once you sit in it. Given my father's weakness—a damaged heart operating at less than one-third capacity—getting out of that couch was taking a major-league effort.*

*Dad was not making much progress. I felt terrible. Knowing he did not have strength to spare, I said, "Dad, you don't have to struggle to stand and pray over me with these friends."*

*"John," my father answered, "I'm not struggling to stand, I'm struggling to kneel."*

*I was overwhelmed. Some statements are so profound they take awhile to sink in; others hit you with the force of a nuclear explosion, and I thought my father's words might vaporize me on the spot. I had a thousand reflections about that statement in the first half second, as if my father's insight had suddenly upgraded my mind from a 286 to a Pentium processor.*

*Buried in my thoughts was a good measure of shame, but it was good shame, the kind of shame that arises when you realize you have vastly underestimated the character of someone or his actions. It is so much more noble to kneel than to stand.*

*It was wonderful that everybody else in the room had taken valuable time out of their day to be with me and to stand and pray for me. But I became keenly aware that my father was operating not out of mere generosity or benevolence. He was conveying a message of eternal value and impact.*

*He as not struggling to stand, he was struggling to kneel.*

*I was taken back to those early mornings half a century before when I slipped underneath my father and joined him on his knees. He prayed then that we would do noble things. Now, still on his knees, he was taking me there.*

---

EDITOR'S NOTE: John Ashcroft was sworn into the Senate on January 4, 1995. His father died that night. This excerpt reprinted by permission of Thomas Nelson, Inc., Nashville, TN, from the book entitled *Lessons from a Father to His Son,* copyright date 1998 by John Ashcroft. 

---

Stronger than all the false prophets trying to undermine our families, exerting an influence far more lasting than all the satanic forces aligned against our homes are the simple goodness and the quiet faith of godly fathers.

One scriptural requirement of an elder is that "he must have proper authority in his own household and be able to control and command the respect of his children" (1 Timothy 3:4-5, Phillips). Godly fathers who fit this description are the church's finest answer to the enemies of the family in any age.

*Rise up, O men of God!*
*Have done with lesser things;*
*Give heart and soul and mind and strength*
*[Thus] to serve the King of kings.*

CHAPTER THIRTEEN

# BUILT ON ROCK: HOMES THAT LAST

*Every one then who hears these words of mine and does them will be like a wise man who built his house upon the rock; and the rain fell, and the floods came, and the winds blew and beat upon that house, but it did not fall, because it had been founded on the rock. And every one who hears these words of mine and does not do them will be like a foolish man who built his house upon the sand; and the rain fell, and the floods came, and the winds blew and beat against that house, and it fell; and great was the fall of it* (Matthew 7:24-27).

Dysfunctional.
Dismembered.
Dissonant.
Disturbed.
Discombobulated.

How many more "dis-" words can you think of to describe the distressed families that live all around us today?

Although it seems to have slowed a bit in recent years, homes in modern America are still coming apart at an alarming rate.

And all the people caught in these domestic meltdowns—both the young and the old—come away from these disasters damaged down deep inside. Far too often these hurting souls become "carriers." Like Typhoid Mary. Many survivors of a home-wreck spread the social germs of anger and distrust and alienation in the schools and churches and offices they populate.

Who can begin to calculate the price we pay each year as a nation when so many of our homes self-destruct?

Late one Friday afternoon last summer I caught a Southwest Airlines flight home from Houston. I was shocked to see the number of kids traveling alone, shuttling from one parent to another to comply with some sort of court-ordered kid-sharing divorce settlement.

And that was just one flight out of hundreds in the air at that hour.

All over our land innocent kids were acting out that same role, their weekends and their lives all the time up in the air because their parents cannot behave as responsible, moral adults who know how to keep a promise.

As we flew northward that day, I studied the faces of those youngsters and wondered which ones were glad to be getting away from one parent and which ones were dreading the coming weekend because the mother or father who would meet them at the end of our flight still practiced the same bad habits that had destroyed their home in the first place.

I sat there in Row 7 and wondered if the parents who were swapping those kids realized what a terrible toll their adult failure was exacting on their offspring.

## HOMES THAT WILL LAST

We must learn again in America to build homes that last.

To borrow our Lord's memorable parable, we must learn to build homes on solid rock instead of shifting sand.

Storms will come to batter our families. In this fallen world they are inevitable.

The winds of tragedy will howl and the floods of failure and frustration will descend upon our homes to assault and test the foundations they are built on. Heartache and hardship are in store for all of us.

We must learn to build homes that are strong enough to endure on the hardest days.

What are the bedrock foundations that will keep our homes intact even in tough times? Can we identify safe terrain on which to construct our families?

If you plan to build an expensive structure on Galveston swamp land or near a Texas panhandle playa lake, your first step should be to hire an experienced engineer to study the soil samples and recommend the sort of foundation that will keep your building intact.

Let me try to fill that role for you. Let me serve as your spiritual engineer and specify some of the essential components of a foundation that will keep a family in one piece on today's shifting soil.

*Integrity*

Honesty seems to be in short supply these days.

My friend Gordon Bickham worked for the same company for 28 years. All those years they treated him great. They convinced Gordon and most of his fellow workers that theirs was the finest company on earth, so fine in fact that they should invest most of their 401K funds in that company's stock. Gordon retired with the secure feeling that his long years of labor and savings would provide amply for his last years.

Gordon was more fortunate than many Enron employees. When he retired, he decided to spread his risk by investing some of his savings elsewhere. Then came the sickening news that hundreds of hard working people like Gordon had been ripped off by company executives and gold-plated auditors whose massive shell game collapsed.

Stock certificates once worth hundreds of thousands of dollars today hang on Gordon's wall, now barely worth the paper they are printed on—mute evidence of the high price of dishonesty.

For several generations now we Americans have been discarding the values that made our country great. In our nation's earliest days, even the leaders who were not confessing Christians still were for the most part men of high honor. They possessed an integrity that was a hangover from the strong Christian faith of their ancestors.

"I cannot tell a lie," George Washington says in the apocryphal tale about that defunct cherry tree. The story may not be a true one, but Washington's real words always were. His contemporaries honored him as a man of unimpeachable integrity.

People like that are increasingly hard to find in our land.

IRS officials estimate that our government gets swindled out of $195 billion every year by taxpayers who lie on their tax returns.

Do you remember when the teacher who penalized over half her class for plagiarizing their research papers was herself reprimanded by local school officials? They sided with the dishonest students. The veteran teacher resigned in disgust.

Cheating has become a way of life. Last year 74 percent of the U.S. high school students surveyed admitted to "serious test cheating"—

more than double the percentage who confessed the same sin in 1969.

In today's world the prevalent philosophy seems to be, "Why tell the truth when a lie will make you look better?"

Anyone who has trouble explaining why the truth is always preferable to a lie should talk to the patients of the Kansas pharmacist who sold cancer patients diluted drugs at full-strength prices, thereby dooming many of them to die.

Anyone who wonders why telling the truth is our only tenable option should count the lives needlessly lost in crashes after maintenance and operations records allegedly were doctored for the V-22 Osprey. Or they should talk to the families of the people on that Air Florida flight that crashed in the Everglades after cargo manifests were falsified.

Most lies have bad consequences. If lives are not lost and companies destroyed by them, at the very least deceit destroys trust and poisons relationships.

"Do not lie," is Number Nine of the famous Ten Commandments. God included it for a reason. Nothing short of total integrity can provide a proper foundation for your home.

My own father was a strict disciplinarian. I recall only too clearly that he warmed up my bottom over a host of minor transgressions. But my dad made it abundantly clear that two offenses were guaranteed to get me into far more trouble than I wanted to deal with.

The unpardonable sin was to sass my mother. She was to receive total respect from us kids at all times. He made sure that she did.

Equally unpardonable was to tell a lie. The few times we were tempted to shade the truth to cover up some minor transgression convinced us never to try it again. For the punishment for dishonesty was many times worse than that for any other sin.

Today I gratefully honor my parents for upholding such standards when they raised me. I was a creative brat, entirely too prone to fabricate a fanciful tale to explain my misdeeds. Today I know that without my parents' consistent, unshakable insistence on truth, I might well be headed to jail with the Enron guys.

Make truth the currency of your home.

Make sure that your spouse and your kids can always bank on your words without ever having to question the veracity of what you say or who you are.

Healthy families don't play games. They don't lie. They don't try to deceive or leave false impressions. As nearly as possible they're up front with each other. What you see is what you get. You'll find out that life is so much easier if you play by those rules.

Being able to trust each other totally is the bedrock, indispensable foundation for a happy, lasting home.

*Morality*

Christian marriage counselors across the nation agree that most families who come to them have conflicts over 1) money, 2) alcohol or drugs, or 3) sex. A post-mortem of a collapsed home usually will reveal a complex combination of all three factors.

In traditional Protestant wedding ceremonies both the bride and groom pledge their sexual faithfulness. "Do you promise to keep yourself only for your husband (or your wife) for the rest of your life?" the minister asks. And the bride or groom answers with the famous, "I do."

Most marriages in America today would survive if both mates kept that simple promise.

But we live in the age of the coed work force. We throw healthy, attractive, desirable males and females together for long hours in close quarters—side by side in the same patrol car or fire station bunkhouse, shoulder to shoulder on battleships or jet fighters. Then we seem surprised when the marriages of municipal workers and military personnel fall apart at alarming rates.

Immorality is nothing new. We humans are sexual by nature and we have never done a very good job of controlling this part of us. In wiser generations we admitted this weakness and set up sensible social structures to protect us from ourselves.

But today our homes are terribly vulnerable to the threat of immorality.

In the name of entertainment we immerse our hearts and minds night after night in the raw lust of shows like the CBS Survivors series or the raunchy stuff on HBO. Then we wonder why it's hard to behave at the office.

With the flick of a switch and the click of three keys any one of us can defile our computer screens with the vilest pornography known to man. Thus we may fuel sexual fantasies that far too often spill over into real life. Few families can survive that kind of pollution.

We don't have to be puritanical or prudish to recognize the real danger immorality poses to our homes. "Blessed are those who hunger for righteousness," Jesus said at the beginning of his famous sermon. A commitment to right living is one key to real, lasting happiness in our homes.

*Responsibility*

I confess that the third foundation component I suggest for a home that lasts is painfully devoid of Hollywood glamour. It will never make headlines or kick off the 6 o'clock news. But no home will survive long without it. I am talking about everyday, ordinary responsibility.

They don't pin medals on guys who go to work every morning, who come home on time every night, and who bring a paycheck home without fail every month to pay the bills. But it takes that kind of basic dependability for a home to survive.

Nobody makes heroes of ladies who often bring home their own paychecks in addition to cooking meals, washing clothes, sweeping floors, feeding pets, taxiing kids, chairing the PTA, and putting up with a husband. But home life craters quickly, doesn't it, if mama neglects many of these simple responsibilities?

Responsibility may be the most underrated virtue of them all. In homes where every person fills his or her assigned role predictably and without much hassle, we tend to take each other for granted and just assume that this is the way all homes operate.

They should. But, sadly, it's not so. On the average city block, you would not have to knock on many doors to find a home where the dishes are dirty, the clothes are dirty, the floors are dirty, and the kids are dirty. All the normal duties in that home are being neglected, and often few of the bills are being paid. A home like this is always at risk, because nobody wants to live like that.

In that original Christian church on the pagan island of Crete, the young wives and mothers were taught that they could present a winsome Christian message simply by tending to basic family responsibilities. The older Christian women trained the younger ones "to love their husbands, to love their children, to be discreet, chaste, homemakers, good, obedient to their own husbands" (Titus 2:4-5, NKJV). In this way, the apostle Paul told them, they could "adorn the doctrine of God our Savior."

Do you want to fortify your home for the stormy times? Start off by vacuuming the carpet. Clean up the clutter. Cook good meals. In other words, be responsible. Every day. Few things matter more to the permanence of your home.

*Faith*

We will run out of space here before we can identify all the elements of a solid, durable foundation for your family. But the final underpinning I recommend for your home covers lots of ground.

Any home that hopes to survive must be established on faith.

All around us homes are crumbling because the people in them tried to build on flimsy substitutes. Instead of faith, some families try to build on financial success. Others base everything on their professional achievements. I even know some families who base their entire existence on how much fun they can have at the fishing hole, at the racetrack, on the ski slopes, or on the ball field.

None of these substitutes are bad things. None of them are illegal or immoral. But neither are they substantial enough to support family relationships that stand strong when the rain falls and the floods come and the winds blow and beat upon their house.

Several years ago my colleague Ron Highfield wrote this testimony about his turbulent adolescence:

> I have often wondered what pulled me through those teen years and instilled faith in me. I believe it was one thing. I never doubted for one second that my dad believed in God from the top of his head to the bottom of his feet! He attended church

every time the doors were opened. That impressed upon me that my relationship with God was not simply a matter of convenience. No cheap grace! (By the way, I doubt if children can understand the logic of our "freedom" not to go to church. It probably communicates that church, and therefore God, is of secondary importance.)

I believe that my dad allowed Christ to touch every area of his life. As he went about his day, he sang or whistled gospel songs. He would discuss the Scriptures or church life as we worked together. I never heard God's name taken in vain or a dirty joke come out of his mouth.

He wanted me to go to college, but I never got the impression that my education was nearly so important to him as my being a committed Christian. In short, I could deny every "abstract" witness to God, but I could not get away from this one life lived in the power and presence of God!

Ron's father chose the right foundation for his family. Nothing short of Almighty God and his eternal promises can see us safely through life's storms.

## THE ONLY RIGHT OPTION

Do you remember the declaration Joshua made to his people shortly before he died?

Faithfully he had led the nation of Israel through hard days of struggle and war to gain a place in the Promised Land. Now the war was over and the land was at rest. And the people, who had stayed marvelously focused all through the long campaign, now had the leisure to let their faith and interests wander from the God who had given them victory.

"Choose this day whom you will serve," old Joshua challenged his people. He acknowledged that they had many alternatives—not all of them safe or wise. But he resolutely declared, "As for me and my family, we will serve the Lord."

You and I face the same choice in our own day. On every hand are tantalizing options, tempting us to replace the church and the Scriptures and the Lord with the temporary pleasures and the deceptive securities of the world.

The substitutes will work just fine as long as the sun shines and gentle breezes blow. While stock market gains are solid and your health is intact, while all your kids are behaving and your bosses think you're great—in halcyon times like that your home doesn't really need a foundation. When the winds of life are favorable, you can construct your family on any of this world's temporary material, and it will stand up deceptively fancy and fine. Like the house built on the sand.

But when the storms come, it will be obvious who listened to the Lord.

"BUT IF SERVING THE LORD
SEEMS UNDESIRABLE TO YOU,
THEN CHOOSE FOR YOURSELVES
THIS DAY WHOM YOU WILL SERVE,
WHETHER THE GODS
YOUR FOREFATHERS SERVED
BEYOND THE RIVER,
OR THE GODS OF THE AMORITES,
IN WHOSE LAND YOU ARE LIVING.
BUT AS FOR ME AND MY HOUSEHOLD,
WE WILL SERVE THE LORD"

–Joshua 24:15, NIV

# ABOUT THE AUTHOR

GENE SHELBURNE has ministered in Amarillo, Texas, to the same congregation of God's people for over 35 years. His weekly religious column is published in several newspapers. He is Senior Editor of *The Christian Appeal*, a monthly devotional magazine now in its 41st year. Every morning he teaches the academic Bible course in a nearby public high school, and he is active in many aspects of community leadership and life. He and his wife of 44 years, Nita, have raised a family of three children and twelve grandchildren, all of them faithful in the Lord's service. His earlier books include *The God Who Puts Us Back Together* and *Expect the Light!*


2310 Anna Street
Amarillo, TX 79106
806-352-8769
Fax 806-356-9680
GeneShel@aol.com